LIFE ON A CAROUSEL

a non-diplomatic memoir

LAUREL PARDY

Order this book online at www.trafford.com
or email orders@trafford.com

Most Trafford titles are also available at major online book retailers.

Printed in Victoria, BC, Canada.

ISBN: 978-1-4269-0921-4

*Our mission is to efficiently provide the world's finest, most comprehensive
book publishing service, enabling every author to experience success.
To find out how to publish your book, your way, and have it available
worldwide, visit us online at www.trafford.com*

Trafford rev. 12/09/2009

 www.trafford.com

North America & international
toll-free: 1 888 232 4444 (USA & Canada)
phone: 250 383 6864 ♦ fax: 812 355 4082

LIFE ON A CAROUSEL

Also by Laurel Pardy

A Lady of Lunenburg

with no regret for the roads not taken

One of the obligations of older age is to share a few hard learned grains of wisdom that might be of use to those who follow. Being neither old nor wise, I abjure any claims to wisdom but gladly share thoughts and pleasures I have had along the way to here, here referring to the phase between retirement at home and a retirement home. Not old age yet but certainly older aged and aware that there are fewer years ahead of me than behind me.

Over those years behind me I occasionally recorded some of the events and ideas and learnings that occurred. Many have been pre-published in *bout de papier*, the Journal of the Canadian Foreign Service. With their permission, I have collected them and some others so that I may share them with readers outside the foreign service.

Déjà vu, plus ça change and all that.

the strength of bamboo
lies in its flexibility

While floundering around in the wake of my husband's roving diplomatic career, I have managed to see a lot of the world, meet some wonderful and inspiring people in low places and high and, not least, shared many unforgettable meals and experienced a few unforgettable moments. I know that travelling as a diplomat protected me from many of life's rougher edges. It took some manipulating to move outside that official circle and participate in ordinary life abroad. Diplomatic life gave me access and opportunity for learning, meeting and accomplishing things I could not have done otherwise: opportunity to talk with experts, academics; access to people who could get things done, grant permission or donate funds; organize funding or supplies for needy organizations and programs. Being able to support small local initiatives was one of the greatest pleasures of having a certain status. It was the times when we could step outside our official role, escape on a journey of our own that remain the most memorable. Balance between public and private life was crucial to family cohesion and harmony.

Welcoming guests and the preparation of meals are a common thread among people everywhere. The giving and receiving of hospitality—I'm not referring to the official intergovernmental kind, although that may have a use as well—is innate to every society, group, tribe and nation. I have had some memorable meals in unexpected places.

Women connect over food and family. Men get to eat and benefit. Safety and shelter, food and feeding, love and nurture: these are always women's concerns through a fruitful life as well as disasters, epidemics or political turmoil. When women cannot provide basic necessities for their families, a society is in collapse. Refugee camps, war zones, disaster aftermath are unnatural human collections but even there I have seen acts of kindness and the sharing of meager resources. Five star restaurant or village hut, both have offered memorable meals.

Memorable moments can also occur in unexpected places. I'm referring to those moments when you sense you are on the cusp of some great understanding, a moment when a larger truth is about to be revealed if you could but grasp it. For me it is always accompanied by the awareness of how small a single person is—me—in the face of a great vastness, whether it be the North Atlantic stretching out to the horizon, the immensity of the Himalayan Mountain range, the implacable forces of a seething caldera or an impenetrable black night lit by a dome of northern lights. The greatest immensity is time, time stretching backward and forward beyond human comprehension. There have been a few moments when I felt myself to be in the flow of time, part of the endless stream, part of eternity. Unplanned and fleeting, they have engraved themselves on my memory like light on a negative, there to be recalled when I become too smug at my own achievements.

Food for the body, food for the soul. Not new concepts but I keep seeking for the perfect recipe.

The reference to bamboo? Ah, that refers to the need to bend and adapt to life's winds.

The episodes captured in the included articles have not been updated. They reflect the times in which they were written; however, a brief historic perspective is provided for clarity where needed.

INDIA : 1969-1972

My love and I met at university—a Maritime university with a strong Baptist tradition of propriety—and the only place we could be alone was always outdoors and always freezing. On one such bone numbing night we were huddled together on a set of secluded stairs behind University Hall talking about life and things when he asked me if I liked to travel. Anyplace had to be warmer than where we were, so I assured him that I was up for plenty of travel. At this point in time, he had been around the world and I had been to Quebec City. As he was a man with a plan and I was a master drifter, it was natural that I just floated along in his wake. Flotsam on life's ocean.

One thing leads to another and five years later two singles had become a pair and a pair had become four. And that four, the youngest barely two months old, were on their way to their first foreign service posting in the world's most exotic country, India.

What I knew about India was right up there with angels on the head of a pin. I thought it was hot and full of people who ate curry. That was true but it was much much more. At that point of my life, I was overwhelmed with the complexity of caring for two babies, packing up our belongings, purchasing the necessities for diplomatic life and moving to the other side of the globe. The idea of an ayah, an Indian nanny, to help care for our babies sounded pretty good to me. The only thing I knew was that if two hundred million women could bring up

1

their children in India, so could I. Provided, of course, the cartons of infant formula arrived.

This was the time of Indira, idealist, canny campaigner, daughter of privilege and politics. India was proudly independent, determined on self sufficiency, still more ancient than modern but struggling to educate its people and take its place in the world beside the other great nations. It still needed foreign aid but it longed to be an equal, not a recipient.

The Canadian High Commission remained old fashioned with offices spread around town in old buildings in old suburbs and small enough that everyone knew everyone else. We all watched out for each other. India was considered a medium level hardship posting. There was a small commissary shared with the Australians, other than that we lived on the Indian market. Canadian Forces planes occasionally flew in small cargoes of essentials such as flour and laundry detergent, Campbell's tomato soup and cartons of canned tuna. There was no housing compound. Except for the High Commissioner and the Trade Commissioner, we all lived in rented accommodation about the city, in middle class neighbourhoods alongside Indian professionals and a scattering of other foreigners. I shopped in the local bazaars and braved the early morning meat markets, the Hindu ones for pork and chicken, the Muslim ones for lamb and goat. There were many worse postings. As I recall, at that moment, Kinshasa was considered the least desirable.

India was a kaleidoscope of sights, sounds and smells. A country of contrasts. Red silk and gold jewellery, rags and leprosy, savoury aromas and stinking excrement, ruined palaces and atomic reactors, incredible wealth and abject poverty. I learned that whatever I said about India, it was true. The dichotomies that unsettled the Western mind fazed not the more subtle sub-continental one.

India was my first experience with ancient history. A Tibetan woman showing me her wares apologized because the statue in which I was interested was only 600 years old, not really a worthy item for worthy memsahib. On a trip to Madurai, I was allowed to touch a Shiva shrine that had been in continuous worship for over 2500 years. Back home a hundred years was old and two hundred, ancient.

At some point I started to write short articles to remind myself of certain experiences and to share my life with my family back in Canada. Partly I wrote them so that I could understand the life I was living and my reaction to it. It was an intense time. I hope I came away wiser than when I arrived.

Old Manali

In 1970, Manali was not a trekker's destination. It was a little mountain village of interest only as the last village before the mountain pass into Leh, now the Leh District in the state of Jammu and Kashmir, India, and thence into China. Refugees from Tibet came into India this way. There were no hotels, restaurants or even proper hostels. Foreigners were viewed politely but with curiosity. However, in memory of a relative who had fought and died with the British Columbia Rangers, there were several Canadian style log cabins and a small lodge to welcome any who come to admire and walk the mountains.

India's relations with Pakistan and China were strained, conflict over Kashmir's borders was on-going and military personnel in the mountain passes were alert and suspicious. We were young, several of the men were bearded, our clothes were casual and we drove an old red and white VW van. We fit the profile for drug seeking overlanders, hippies driving from Europe to Asia, not the clean living diplomats we were and this was an area of unrest. We never felt ourselves to be in danger, except from the roads and other drivers, but we had no desire to test the tempers of the authorities, so we kept our demeanour sober, our behaviour circumspect and our celebrations private—well, maybe a wee dram and a few fire crackers.

Friends Colony, New Delhi, January, 1971

Ever wake up one morning and think, "If I have to spend one more day in this place, I won't be responsible for the consequences?"

Sixteen months of unremitting Indian heat, dust and crowds have taken their toll. I am desperate for brisk dawns and sweater evenings. I want to sleep snuggled under a quilt and to stand in front of a fire with warm hands and cold cheeks.

I want to go camping. I want to build a fire and roast marshmallows. I want to see evergreens, hear mountain streams and throw a beefsteak on the BBQ. I want to breathe cold air. I want to be alone for an hour. Privacy is almost non-existent in our Indian world.

I do not want to attend another "official event" for at least a hundred years. Diwali and Christmas are both social seasons and this year they came within a few weeks of each other. Diwali, the festival of "rows of lights", is celebrated for three or more consecutive days and is the most important of all Hindu festivals, usually occurring in October or November. In simple terms, it celebrates the victory of good over evil, of light over dark. The invitations had stacked up at the rate of three or four a day and we were entertained to exhaustion.

In addition to its deserts and plains India has mountains, especially in the northern territory where the massive Himalayas separate India from the Tibetan Plateau. Among the foothills are valleys accessible by road, a few anyway. One of them is the Kulu Valley which lies north-south along both sides of the Beas River. At the end of the valley is the little village of Manali. Beyond Manali the road becomes a set of near-vertical switchbacks up to the Rohtang Pass and the dirt road to Leh, the capital of the Himalayan kingdom of Ladakh. Off the road past Manali is Banon's Cabins, a rustic log cabin retreat on an escarpment overlooking the headwaters of the Beas. These cabins become the trip destination for eight home-hungry Canadians.

The 570 km drive will take two days. We plan to overnight in Mandi, a small village just into the foothills, 465 km north of New Delhi. We have made arrangements to stay the night in the dak bungalow, a remnant of colonial days when travelling British administrators kept a string of houses permanently ready for them as they travelled about India. These days they are used as basic inns. There are charpoys, the ubiquitous rope beds, and mosquito nets. We had been warned to bring bed rolls, soap and towels and insecticide. The trick with the charpoys is to gently carry them outside, away from your bungalow, and drop them firmly on the hard ground; this knocks out the bed bugs from the cracks and interstices in the woven rope. The cots are then carried back into the room where each leg of the charpoy is placed into tin cans containing a strong solution of Dog Brand phenol so that the bugs will not crawl back home. The room is thoroughly sprayed with Flit, a DDT compound, and mosquito nets are dropped to the floor and lifted only just long enough for you to get into bed.

For dinner the chowkidar, watchman, catches and kills a hen which he takes home for his wife to cook, after which he carries it back along with a few chapattis, flat breads made from soft Indian wheat flour, on tin plates for our dinner. Indian families travel with all their food, dishes, linens and a full staff of servants to scrub the bungalow and cook their meals. We are poor naïve specimens but he does his best for us.

It is little over a hundred kilometres to Manali but it takes most of the next day. The road climbs steadily through largely cedar forest in a series of switchbacks that overlook the Beas River. Construction of the Beas-Sutlej link is underway and the roads are gravel, widened to allow passage of the trucks that carry in and out all the necessities for the building of the hydro electric project. Our views of the Beas are hindered by the number of times we close our eyes to avoid contemplating the results of a plunge down the shifting gravel ledge along which we rattle. I only learn later that our driver is fearless only because he tops up his courage from a handy bottle each time we stop to admire the view. So much for an abstemious Muslim. We had brought him as guide and translator, however, after this trip he goes firmly back to his position as our cook.

As we leave the picturesque village of Kulu for the last short leg of our trip to Manali and our mountain retreat, trite hyperbole takes over—the deodar cedars and pine trees rear up in triumphant splendour; the mountains soar in purple majesty; the log cabins glow in warm welcome…

For a homesick Canadian, the rushing stream with its stone grist mill and water wheel, the fat-tailed sheep in the lush meadow, the soaring evergreen trees and the cold pure mountain air make the sweaty, unpredictable drive worthwhile.

It is the season of Diwali, the Festival of Lights, and we have brought firecrackers to celebrate. We have brought toilet paper and soap, matches and lanterns, coffee and salt and chappati flour, bedrolls and books. What we haven't brought is firewood or meat for the stew pot. These we had assumed would be readily available. No, no. The villagers collect their own firewood in the forest and slaughter their own hens and goats. We finally locate a bag of coal and a kilo of goat meat. From these we learn two lessons: never let the fire go out and start the curry the day before. Goat has a long cooking time—we chew the meat, suck the flavour out and leave the residue on the plate. We also do not understand the impact of cooking at 2200 m above sea level. No hard boiled eggs. It takes over an hour to get the fire going to make the coffee which is appalling because the water boils at a lower temperature.

Drawn by the lure of snow on the mountains farther up the road, we obtain permission from the local military commander to drive to the beginning of the Rohtang Pass. We would be allowed to drive to the beginning of the Pass, no farther. Any farther and we would be on our way to Leh, a forbidden destination unless special military permission is granted. Anyway, out of caution we would not subject our old van to days of perilous roads and high mountain passes.

The cluster of structures scattered about the valley floor are the yurts of Tibetan refugees who have festooned every tall tree with strings of prayer flags that hang like lines of tatty washing from treetop to treetop, twenty five, thirty metres up. How did they do that? The only answer is that they must climb the evergreen trees. I am impressed at this determined manifestation of their faith.

The highway is military grade dirt and gravel, welcome, but it is not for local traffic. This close to the Chinese border, it is for military traffic. The only barrier is a rope looped around a couple of stones on either side of the road with a few prayer flags tied onto it. We did see one commercial bus cross over with a few passengers.

The local people do not own vehicles but climb, not the winding road, but the foot paths straight up the mountainside and cross the ravines on narrow rope bridges. We try an easy one during our tea stop, close to the swiftly rushing water and only a few metres across. There must be a technique but we do not have it. We dip our hands in the water; it is painfully, glacially cold.

Two hours and thirty-five kilometres of tortuous turns later find us at the top of the pass and five hundred metres from the snow line. We start up the gentle slope to attempt a few snowballs only to collapse after a few metres. How ignorant we are of altitude. New Delhi sits ten metres above sea level, our cabins are at 2200 metres but the top of the pass is at 4500 metres. The ignominy of it all is that little boys have run up the mountain paths beside our van and happily play chase as we gasp for air. They offer to run up and bring us back some snow. I hold out my hand and one places some in it. He laughs and darts out of the way as I toss it at him.

After I catch my breath, I walk over and stand alone at the edge of the mountainside, so that I cannot see the others. The silence is absolute. No birds, no trees, no cars, no habitations. There is only the soundless vigilance of a stone prayer cairn erected by Tibetans who believe that their gods live in these mountains. I understand why they believe this to be so. As I gaze at the serried rows of snow-capped peaks that stretch to every horizon, I can believe it, too. Man could not conceive nor construct anything so audacious, so humbling. It would take a force beyond our understanding or control.

Finally, cold and hunger force us off the mountain and back to our campsite where a delectably pungent lamb korma dinner awaits us. The aroma is pure seduction.

The rice is fluffy, the chapatis are tender but the lambs of mountain sheep have to be tough, and it is a characteristic they refuse to relinquish, even on the dinner plate. Still, it is my thirtieth birthday dinner and we wash it down with bottles of Bulgarian white wine brought for that purpose.

The next day, I clutch my jacket around me and wander about, collecting huge evergreen cones, dabbling in the glacial water of a shallow brook and wallowing in nostalgia—and vowing never to drink at altitude again. However, behind the familiar facade lurks the reality of another culture. The differences tiptoe up on me and for a time I resist their intrusion. I do not want to take off my blinkers but India, as usual, refuses to be ignored. It simply shoves its dichotomies in one's face.

The cabins offer western beds, flush toilets and electric heaters but nothing on which to cook except a recalcitrant clay oven. The rooms are clean but a friendly rat keeps vigil on my headboard and strokes my forehead with its tail as I sleep off the white wine. In the market one can buy beautiful wool shawls but meat only when there are extra animals that owners can afford to slaughter, coca cola but no charcoal. The stalls have little to offer; some chapati flour, cooking oil and salt, a few expensive onions, carrots and potatoes, tumeric, dried chilis and tea are the luxuries that the people here work long hours to afford. Beautiful children wave gaily and both men and women climb the steep trails with towering loads but are old at forty, or thirty. Beauty and ugliness and no attempt to hide either. No wonder the Indian mind has no difficulty with duality, the country is built on it.

One thing is the same though. A big, friendly golden Labrador retriever takes up residence in our kitchen and enjoys the luxury of our tough leftover meat. A mooch pooch is a mooch pooch the world over.

The Old Story Teller

Nizamuddin, New Delhi, India, 1970

I remember his eyes, calm and steady as they gaze through the bottle-bottom spectacles. When he looks at you, you do not see the wrinkled face or the dusty, once-white rags that flutter about his emaciated limbs.

In another incarnation he might have been a miniature St. Nicholas but, in this existence, he is an old story-teller, begging out his life on the teeming streets of New Delhi. He is a tiny man, shorter than my five foot two, fragile-looking under his load of cloths. His garments could hardly be called clothes, yet they wrap him round in familiar comfort; garments by day, bed clothes by night.

He carries a small bundle, a bamboo walking stick and a black umbrella. The bundle contains his life's possessions, the stick gives steadiness to his faltering steps, and the umbrella provides a roof against the sun and rain.

He is waiting for me one day, sitting quietly on my front steps. Usually the gate to our yard is locked so that beggars cannot wander in off the streets. I go over to shoo him away and instead bring him tea — hot, milky, and full of sugar — the way old men like it. In doing so, I know that I am only encouraging him to return but I have not the heart to refuse such a small thing to someone with such a tenuous hold on life.

Inevitably, he returns. This time my young sons are in the garden and, certain that at the very least he carries lice and tuberculosis, I hurry to bring them inside.

They are seated on the steps at his feet. Only their eyes move as he unfolds a tale of Ram and his search for his beloved Sita. The story is told in the soft, fluid tones of a language they do not know; however, the language is irrelevant, they are enthralled.

Once again, instead of sending him away, I go inside to see to his tea which I make by bringing a generous cup and a half of whole water buffalo milk to a boil and adding a soup spoon of black tea leaves, an inch of cinnamon bark and a green cardamom pod, crushed. I give it a stir and take the pot off the heat until it stops bubbling. I bring it to a boil again and again take it off the heat. I add two soup spoons of dark unrefined sugar and return it to a boil and then remove it from the heat. I pour it into his chipped enamel mug and let the tea leaves settle. It takes him an hour to sip his way through the large enamel mug full of strong chai. He gets to keep the tea leaves; for the rest of the day he has only to pay the chai wallah, tea seller, for the hot water—he already has the tea leaves. A few annas from another customer will pay for the sugar; a few from another will purchase the milk. He owns the mug.

He accepts the tea and some small coins with a slight nod of his head. This is no hand-out; he had rendered his service in the telling of the tale and the payment is his due.

He is a regular visitor during the remainder of our stay in India. It is not necessary to leave the gate unlocked for him and, although I watch, I never see him enter the grounds. I just find him resting patiently in the shade of our porch until someone takes notice of him.

If my boys are not there to provide him with an audience, he tells his stories to the shrubs and flowers so that the tea and the coins can never be called charity. I sometimes see the children from the servant's quarters hiding behind the bushes, listening avidly. They will not come out if I am there, although my sons say they come if they are alone.

I do not regret the coins or the endless cups of sweet tea; however, I will regret forever that I never asked his name. We called him Bubuji— Old Uncle.

New Delhi to Mazar-i-Sharif

Relations between India and Pakistan were at a nadir in the fall of 1971. Sabres were rattling, battalions were being brought up to strength, soldiers were being moved to border regions. In New Delhi, trenches were being dug in the parks to provide shelter from Pakistani bombs, windows were taped and black outs were enforced—not hard since the electricity was often shut down, along with the water supply. India, Pakistan and Afghanistan were less familiar to Canadians than they are now, 37 years later; however, they were infant democracies with unknown nuclear capacity in a time of global cold war. And so, at the behest of the Canadian High Commission, our overland journey from New Delhi in central India to Mazar-i-Sharif in northern Afghanistan included a jolly bit of sleuthing. We were to record numbers of troops on the move, numbers and types of military vehicles, regiment badges, the general mood of officials and so on... East Pakistan was becoming independent Bangladesh and the potential leader, Mujibur Rahman was captured and rumoured to be incarcerated at Attock Fort in West Pakistan. Would we take a look as we drove past?

Afghanistan was not on the Canadian political radar screen at that point and it piqued official attention mainly as a conduit for overlanders—hippies driving painted vans from Europe to Asia seeking enlightenment—and hashish—which they were also seeking as a means to enlightenment. Our interest was mostly in exotic scenery, explorations of little known countryside, purchasing some of the black and red Mazar carpets, and staying out of trouble with the local badmash or hooligans. We reviewed some history, packed extra water and food, a few sweaters and jerry cans of petrol and set off.

We left the children in New Delhi with their ayah and the rest of the house staff. Their nanny, a British trained Christian woman of good sense and character, immigrated to Canada and still, 40 years later, remains a family friend. If war started while we were away, the plan was to abandon our old van in Lahore, fly to the Middle East and from there return to New Delhi. Friends at the High Commission would keep an eye on things.

These were the years of the Cold War, suspicion was high for everything communist, we were forbidden to converse with the Soviets, China was not trusted and most of us were Sino-ignorant, nuclear war seemed a genuine possibility, spying was presumed to be normal activity for diplomats; it was easier then to identify "the enemy".

Day 1: New Delhi

Our departure time is before sunrise, not only is it cooler but our first night is to be in Lahore, Pakistan, some 525 kilometres north along the Grand Trunk Road. Distance is more accurately measured in time than kilometres and it is some 15 hours away. We pick up our travelling companions, Gale and Randy, and start our adventure in buoyant spirits. The first destination is Amritsar, site of the Golden Temple, spiritual home for the world's estimated twenty five million Sikhs. It is 450 km north of New Delhi across the dry, hot, Punjab plain. Punjab is an industrious state and the road is busy, the traffic a mélange of tightly turbaned Punjabis on foot, on bicycle and on bullock carts; gaily painted lorries carrying fruit and cement; military vehicles with canvas covered loads of armed soldiers and farmers laying out their grain harvest on the road to be winnowed by the passing traffic.

We are not travelling incognito. All Canadian High Commission cars are identified with large hand painted license plates emblazoned with diplomatic and Canadian symbols. Fortunately our reputation is in good order and most people wave and smile. Not to mention that we are driving an old red and white Volkswagon van with a sunroof and a tendency to backfire, in other words, a hippie van. The combination confuses some of the officials who do not view this as a proper diplomatic vehicle.

Lunch under a tree beside a canal and on into Amritsar. Like all old cities it is a maze of crowded, narrow unmarked streets. We finally hire a rickshaw wallah who, for 10 rupees, is willing to guide us to the Golden Temple. Later we learn that nobody actually drives to the Golden Temple, they park outside and approach it on foot through the market. However, we plunge into and out of a maze of alleyways and arrive at the site with only a dent in the side from a bullock cart. High noon is not the time to visit but it is the time we have. It is hot; blood boiling, skin searing, eyeball peeling hot. Barefoot we hop over the scorching tiles, admiring the large water pool and pillared colonnades. It is beautiful, open and graceful, its golden tiles and decoration gleaming in the brilliant sun. The central place of prayer is a smaller shrine in the centre of the large square pool reached by a bridge. We are not allowed inside. Occasional bathers dip in the sacred tank but there is not a breath of air due to the high surrounding walls and no relief from the sun glaring off the white marble. Devotees take siestas in the shade of the roofed passages. Idiot Infidels wander about in the noonday sun.

We take the narrow dusty back roads to Ferospore to view the military traffic. No trouble doing that, there are large convoys everywhere, along with supply trucks and tank carriers. The border crossing into Pakistan takes an hour and a half with a minimum of difficulty. Thankful of the privileges of CD plates we watch people remove every item in their baggage followed by their vain attempts to repack. At the moment we are loved by both India and Pakistan and, I hope, Afghanistan.

All fresh produce coming overland from either Pakistan or Afghanistan to India has to pass through Pakistan. Since none of these trucks may come into India, all the fresh fruit for the Indian trade is transferred by hundreds of coolies from Pakistan to hundreds of coolies from India at a single narrow gateway, and then reloaded onto Indian trucks and taken into the cities. At this season, grapes dominate. This transaction is carefully supervised by border police on both sides. The Indian coolies are identified by drab grey kurtas, long loose shirts, and the Pakistani ones wear bright blue.

It is dark when we reach Lahore. After several false starts we locate the Intercontinental Hotel and fall into a hot bath. Gale and I are covered with tiny squashed black flies that had blown in through the open roof of the van.

India is predominantly a Hindu nation; therefore, beef is a non-commodity. Pakistan is predominantly Muslim and beef is occasionally available. And on the hotel menu. Steak dinners all round.

Lahore is a pleasant city, clean and organized. The scooter taxis are decorated with tinsel, garlands and gaudy paintings. There is no square inch of undecorated surface on the lorries. The tongas are well kept and the horses seem healthier than in Delhi. Horns blare and drivers shout. The National Day Memorial is an impressive tower soaring on slender arches. We take the elevator to the top but a heavy haze obscures the view. A quick visit to the Lahore Fort produces the first flat tire of the trip.

Day 2: Lahore, Pakistan

Several hours out of Lahore we leave the plains behind and follow winding roads through low foothills into Islamabad. The terrain is desert-like, low vegetation consisting of sage, stunted trees and a few cactus; low hills cut up with gulches and dry monsoon river beds. Lots of camels in evidence but only one or two villages within sight.

The trip is uneventful and takes little over four hours. We report in at the High Commission first and then stay with friends. Islamabad feels isolated and conversation with us outsiders is eagerly sought. Islamabad is a new city and lacks the character of the older capitol, Karachi. In New Delhi we live in a well-to-do Indian neighbourhood with houses clustered around a central green space called a maidan. All our neighbours with few exceptions are Indian. Here ones neighbours are other foreigners, there is little traffic other than diplomatic cars with drivers; it seems rather sterile.

Day 3: Islamabad, Pakistan

En route to the Afghan border, we pass close by the Attock Fort where Sheikh Mujibur Rahman is rumoured to be incarcerated. It is 101 km west of Islamabad on the left bank of the Indus River. There are many soldiers in the area. We drive circumspectly, no cameras in sight although I sneak a picture through the window from under my shirt. We do not stop. Attock Fort is not a tourist destination today. The entrance is via a narrow suspension bridge across a ravine and is barricaded with heavy razor wire and the soldiers guarding the bridge over the gorge have very sharp looking bayonets on their rifles. Conclusion: maybe there is an important prisoner inside.

We are into the Khyber Pass by 0900. The Khyber Pass, 53 kilometeres long and at its narrowest 3 meters wide, is the easiest land passage through the Hindu Kush mountain range and connects Pakistan with Afghanistan. It has been a major trade route as well as military access route for centuries.

We have to sign in before entering the Khyber and must be out by sundown. It has its own nightlife and we do not wish to be part of it. All local men wear bandoliers and carry one or more guns supported by wicked looking knives—the presence of danger is palpable, although no one is threatening.

The Khyber Pass is as awesome as its reputation. The geology is new, unsmoothed by time, wind and rain, a narrow defile that follows the lower sides of the jagged barren mountains that loom overhead. Perception is distorted and visual distance illusory. It is the only drivable pass, extremely narrow, still not much wider than the camel trail it originally was. For long stretches nothing is green, all is brown, a thousand shades of terracotta. There are no streams or crops to be seen, in a rain, the gullies would become a torrent. The primary colours of the nomadic women's skirts and shawls are in stark contrast and the shiny black tarmac winds on and on.

There are many remains of British sandstone fortifications, tank traps and gun emplacements. The Ali Masjid Fort still sits atop the high isolated pinnacle where it can command both entrances to the pass. There are several large walled villages and a small town called Landi Khotal, commonly referred to as the Smuggler's Bazaar.

The village is a street bazaar huddled in a ravine passing under the road. People crowd the narrow maze of streets; terms like "swashbuckling" and "dark-eyed beauty" come to mind. Gleaming rifles and bandoliers are de rigueur for every man over fourteen. Foreign watches, radios, car parts or whole trucks are for sale at moderate to high prices. If one asks for an item which they do not have, the answer is, "Come back tomorrow; I will get it for you". I buy two water canteens for Sunday outings in the park back in Delhi.

The nomads are migrating to their winter encampments so there are numerous caravans—dogs, hens, burros, camels loaded with the family goods—winding their way along invisible trails. Their black round topped tents are strapped to the camels, chickens are tied by their legs to the top of the load, children walk alongside or ride in mother's arms atop a camel or burro. The women hide their faces occasionally, often ignore you entirely, rarely smile if their man is watching but give Gale and me a flashing glance and quick wave as they pass. The little boys shout and wave, the little girls behave like their mothers. NO pictures please.

The entry into Afghanistan at the northern end of the pass is accomplished with ease, only three quarters of an hour with several stops for stamping of passports and changing of money to pay the tolls.

As we approach Kabul, the road dips into the Kabul Gorge. Jagged, precipitous cliffs rear above us as the road follows the river bed, minutes later we are climbing tortuously up that same cliff in bottom gear. At one point a sharp turn suddenly reveals a brown mud village spilling down a craggy hillside into a mirage-like lake that springs from some unseen source. Nothing else in sight except more hills. Here the colours are endless hues of grey and purple.

We arrive in Kabul by early afternoon and secure rooms at the Kabul Hotel. Many visitors are in town for the King's birthday which will be celebrated tomorrow by a bushkashi tournament. Pronounced bush' ka she, it is an equestrian game in which riders compete to gain control of a goat or calf carcass that has been decapitated and dehooved. Horsemen from one side must scoop up the carcass, ride around a pole or designated marker, reverse course, and drop it into the goal. It has been played across the steppes of Asia since 600 BCE and is considered the forerunner of polo..

Day 4: Kabul, Afghanistan

Early the next morning we visit the Aziz supermarket, small but offering a few imported goods, mostly German in origin, expensive but tempting to someone who has been living in supermarket and import-free India for two years. Strangely enough I buy a tin of sauerkraut, a three-prong fork and Hungarian paprika.

There is no Canadian Embassy here so we are the informal representatives for our country to the Royal Bushkashi Tournament. Our High Commissioner in Islamabad who is responsible for Afghanistan is quite willing for us to do the needful this year. By ten o'clock we are at the bushkashi grounds where we secure our places in the diplomatic section. We are asked frequently for our passes but get by on our diplomatic passports and the help of Mr. Tarzi, the chief of protocol for the MFA. We are seated directly behind the Soviet and French ambassadors. We look them over. The Frenchman is quite neat and dapper; the Soviet is built like a bear wearing a rough heavy wool suit which strains across his shoulders. The Soviet is enthusiastic about the game and repeatedly jumps up and down, waving his arms and shouting. After perfunctory introductions, they ignore us completely. [Remember, these were the years of the frigid cold war, we were forbidden to consort with Soviets or Chinese and, if we did, we had to submit a written report on the event and the conversation.]

The horses are magnificent. I jump over a low wall to take some photographs and land on a pile of fur rugs. Only when I notice the gaping headless necks do I realize I am atop the "balls" prepared for the event. These are the headless calves for the games. A player carries these 150 pound carcasses single handed at full gallop to be dropped into the scoring circle. In the meantime opposing players tear it from his hand, run their horses into him and hit him with a quirt, all at full gallop. The field is a kilometre long by half a kilometre wide and play races back and forth with few rules. Kublai Khan is speculated to have played this game using live captives as "ball".

Surging scrums of plunging horses followed by desperate gallops around the field as the players circle the flags and race for the home circle. Over 10,000 spectators are standing around the roped off field, horses often plunge into this crowd, scattering it momentarily. Three times play is right at our feet. The only women among the spectators are foreigners, no Afghan woman would ever go and, for sure, all the players are men. It is an incredible feat of strength, balance, stamina, and bravado.

The same evening we see "The Horseman" (after the book by Joseph Kessels) at a local cinema, dubbed in Pushtu, excellent photography but not up to the book. Gale and I are the only women in the audience but we are accompanied by men, keep well covered and have no hassle.

Days 5 & 6: Kabul, Afghanistan

The next two days we tramp the Kabul bazaars in search of rugs and sheepskin coats, lapis lazuli and leather goods. We indulge in lamb kebabs and yogurt drinks and purchase a wool sweater each as the cold Afghan winter is approaching.

Day 7: Kabul, Afghanistan

Leave for Mazar-i-Sharif early on a cold morning. Hoar frost lies over the ground, a dust of snow ices the mountains and our breath forms a cloud of vapour. Meanwhile we acquired two passengers, Richard Ingram (college friend of Randy's) and Luis Villota (a photographer for Pan-Am). We stop at a small tea house before entering the 2.6 km long,

3400 m high Salang Tunnel which replaces the perilous climb over the higher Salang Pass. In 1955 Afghanistan and the Soviet Union signed an agreement to initiate joint development of the Salang road, initially via the historic Salang mountain pass route. The tunnel was opened in 1964 and provides a year-round connection from the North and the Soviet Union to Kabul. The tunnel represents the major north-south connection in Afghanistan, cutting travel from 72 hours to 10 hours and saving about 300 km. It reaches an altitude of about 3,400 m and is 2.6 km long. The width and height of the tunnel tube are 7 m. About 1000 vehicles pass through the tunnel daily.

The tea is hot, milky and welcome; the facilities of the new outhouse are also welcome but nowhere near hot. It is a small two-holer cantilevered out over a 1000 m cliff up which the frigid wind of the Hindu Kush sweeps briskly. At least we girls could sit down and ignore the drop; I wonder how the men made out?

In Afghanistan the main road south of Kabul is supported by the Americans and the road north by the Soviets. We joke that they are so wide and excellent because they are built for military vehicles. [In 1979, when the Soviets invaded Afghanistan, it was no longer a joke; in 2008, it is still a military road and it still isn't a joke.]

Beautiful road, spectacular scenery, small hutments in fertile nooks backed by soaring jagged peaks shining gold in the rising sun. Golden leaved trees and little boys catching trout for breakfast in the small river that wanders through the lower level of the pass. The mountain trails look steep even for goats. Once out of the pass we are back down to the desert which stretches to the horizon. Occasional shepherds and brown mud villages. The sheep are lovely fat-tailed ones whose bottoms waggle like an insulted dowager as they hurry down the road. Car engine starts to misbehave but keeps ticking noisily. Reach Mazar at 1700 hours and register at the hotel. The exhilarating drive has taken longer than the predicted seven hours.

The hotel is a former palace fallen on hard times. Much is in ruins, one wing has fallen down, electricity is from a generator which is turned on from sunset until 2100 hours, hot water is from a kettle over an open fire. Its twenty-two rooms share a common bathtub with no plug. It takes an hour to prepare the bath and we draw lots for first dibs. I win. The toilet has its own room but no running water. The sink is in the bedroom also with no plug. We arrange for hot water with the room servant, for toilet flushing with the water bucket boy and are thankful we brought our own toilet paper and camp lantern. Fortunately we also have our own bedding, soap, towels, tub plugs, etc. Food is non-existent but service is polite and adequate. We purchase some flat bread from a roadside seller and scrounge fried eggs from one of the staff. The only other guests are two elderly women from New York who want to know the status of the World Series—alas, we have no idea.

From a distance the red and black Afghan rugs are beautiful but they seem crude upon closer inspection. Don't find any of the green striped Mazar coats. Fail to locate a shop offering quality goods. Do no shopping.

In the centre of Mazar the Blue Mosque, Hazrat Ali, the mausoleum of Imam Ali, Muhammad's son-in-law, the forth caliph of Islam and the founder of Shiism stands in solitary splendour. Although the workmanship is not as fine as on some others, the geometric patterns are brilliant in stunning blues and yellow, in complete contrast to the monotonous countryside. Each gate is crowded with beggars, diseased and disabled. On the whole we have not been pestered by beggars in Afghanistan. Perhaps after two years in India we have acquired a facial expression that conveys that we will not be intimidated. Non-Muslims are not allowed into the Mosque; Muslim women have their special times to enter. We admire from afar and avoid the aggressive hawkers and touts.

By now it is my turn to be sick after a dinner of kebabs at a dusty roadside tea stall and I retire early. Quite a letdown after the tasty kebabs we'd consumed in the Kabul tea stalls with no resultant revenge.

Day 8: Mazar-i-Sharif, Afghanistan

The next morning a rooster that I hope becomes a tasty dinner starts crowing at 0300 and carries on each half hour until seven o'clock. Our breakfast of fried eggs and flat bread is brought to our rooms on a tray along with a mug of hot strong coffee and evaporated milk. The traditional European service in such extreme conditions is bizarre.

We drive out to Balkh to view the old mosque and fortifications. Balkh is the remains of a great ancient centre for commerce and culture; possible birth and burial place of Zoroaster; burial place of Busephalus,

Alexander the Great's favourite horse; capital city of Alexander the Great, Genghis Khan, Babur and Tamerlane. It is now a dusty village of little distinction but when I remember that it has been in existence for 4500 years I begin to feel its mystery. Some of the ambience survives and, as I sit on top of the old fortification walls of Alexander, I marvel at the history that has passed through this city. The plains stretch out like time and the distant hills still reign majestic against the blue morning sky. Never have I felt such a sense of history and loss of possibilities not realized and of roads not taken.

The car is ailing but we head out for Kabul. The tread peels off one tire; I take Lomatil in generous quantity and quietly curl into a corner of the van. Kebabs rule! There are no pit stops along this route and any likely niche has been discovered by a hundred others before us. However, needs must and I crouch melancholy behind a small rock while a herd of sheep and shepherds meander past.

Kabul again. About half the women in Kabul wear burquas, often over modern dress, occasionally cut short in the front so that their legs show but not their faces, a gesture to tradition. Most main streets in Kabul are wide, some have boulevards, others are mere alleys. Early morning traffic is camels, burros, pushcarts, a few bicycles but the rest of the day is mainly cars. Every corner has a traffic cop and they expect to be obeyed. At one corner, heavy with traffic, a taxi is waved to a halt. When the driver doesn't react fast enough the cop wrenches open the car door, shakes the man and shouts abuse at him. Kabul has both bazaars and stores throughout all the main streets. Stores are small and crowded with prices on a par with Canada. We are all favourably impressed with Kabul. I think the wide streets, orderly traffic and lack of garbage and roadside squatters created a more comfortable ambience for the western mind. But the zoo—oh, my, enough to make one weep.

Day 9: Kabul, Afghanistan

This morning I woke before dawn to the sound of muted wooden camel bells. I sit at the window and watch as a long camel caravan moves sedately along the city street in the morning fog following a path that may have predated the city itself. The camels certainly gave the impression that it is the city that is in the way, not them.

We decide to visit the Bamiyan Valley and spend the day making arrangements. Bamiyan is the site of the world's tallest standing statues of the Buddha. It is an arduous 170 km trek by road and our van is experiencing ill health so we arrange to fly in courtesy Baktar Airlines. They are using a Canadian made Twin Otter although they have just purchased three Yak 40's from the Soviets; however, they are not in service yet.

Day 10: Kabul, Afghanistan

We take off for Bamiyan only an hour late and have a quick flight above continuous mountain ridges and below continuous thunderheads. The next day a large tour is due to fly in—so much for out of the way places. We stay in the yurts, a twenty-five hut complex built for the filming of "The Horsemen", very comfortable rooms with eating facilities at the main hotel building. The food is plain and very edible, remarkable considering the isolation of the valley. I expected to be eating potato stew three meals a day, with tough chapati on the side. It is potato stew but it also contains carrots, onions and lamb. Bamiyan is poor but poverty is relative, they are well off compared to many other villages but there are no luxuries.

We fail to arrange a trip into the Blue Lakes, Band-e-Amir. Disappointment but this gives us more time to see the village and the Buddhas. The Buddhas are impressive but need preservation work if they are to remain. Built in 507 CE, the shorter one at 35m is receiving some care in conjunction with the Indian Archeological Society. The Buddhas have neither forehead nor nose, they were removed on the order of Ghengis Khan in 1221 CE. We climb the path to the top of the larger one, built in 554 CE, measuring 53m in height. Since Bamiyan is about 3000m above sea level we find it a struggle. In fact Gale and I have moments of doubt and take several meditation stops. We feel our way through a dark tunnel, past floor level slits that open onto a 50m drop to the valley floor and emerge on the head of the tallest standing Buddha. Gar sits quite calmly on the edge of Buddha's forehead but I retire to the safely of the tunnel. The view is breathtaking, humbling. We explore a few of the hundreds of surrounding caves. Alas the shortage of public washrooms causes fouling of the floors and we do not investigate further. At one time 20,000 Buddhist monks inhabited this valley; these caves were their cells.

Gar and Randy investigate the smaller Buddha but Gale and I have other plans. We have arranged to go horseback riding. We rent horses that are bushkashi trained but are now too old to play. They prance about like yearlings as far as I can see. The tack is mainly rope. The halter is tied intricately around their head and becomes the reins, the stirrups are also of rope tied to the saddle and the saddle is exaggerated western style with a large pommel and high back. It is carved from wood with a gaily coloured blanket thrown over it. Comfortable enough. Our guide is an ex-player of indeterminate age and an efficient rider. We are not but we have a grand time. The air is fresh and cool, the deciduous trees are in yellow fall colour and it is like home. We sleep dreamless that night.

The valley is beautiful. A small river meanders down the centre of it, the trees resemble poplars with the leaves turning gold, the houses are mud over mud brick with high walled courtyards, the lanes wander between the walls and people share the right of way with the cows and the burros. The air is unpolluted and crisp. Potatoes and corn are being harvested, sage brush is being collected for the winter fires. Milk must be scarce as there is none served with tea or coffee. Judging by the animals I see, goat's milk should be available but maybe it is not the season.

Day 11: Bamiyan, Aghanistan

We leave on one of the three tourist planes that arrive today. Today everyone is inbound, no reservation needed for the outbound.

Day 12: Kabul, Afghanistan

Stay in Kabul two more nights. Still seeking one of the elaborately embroidered sheepskin coats, preferably one that does not stink. Even Abdullah's coat factory disappoints. Leather is tanned with the same ancient methods, spit sprayed and willow rod beaten. Again the finished product is crude, continually disappointed by this. Drive out to Paghman, a lovely little hillside village full of autumn leaves and several running brooks. Go to the Bagh-e-Bala for lunch. Elegant, if rudely painted, building with high domed ceilings, steeply curved and heavily carved archways. During this stay in Kabul we are blessed with Akbar, our room boy. Obsequious and highly scented he is unforgettable and, we suspect, highly sexed. Gale and I go nowhere in the hotel alone.

Day 13: Kabul, Afghanistan

Coming down from Kabul we pass many nomadic camel caravans moving to winter quarters. The flocks of goats and sheep travel in separate convoys tended by young men and boys. Only babies or the very old ride, everyone else walks. Plenty of sheep dogs but few horses. The women wear full red skirts, long blouses and wrap themselves in wide black shawls. The ornaments are heavy silver necklaces, bracelets and hair ornaments studded with turquoise and semi-precious gems. None seem to wear the blue lapis lazuli stone, perhaps it is too expensive now that it has become a commercial tourist item. Also this is rather far from Kandahar where it is mined. These women do not cover their faces and they smile frequently. They have a very straight carriage, high cheekbones, prominent noses and flashing dark eyes. The young girls are very pretty but they age quickly.

About 160 km out of Kabul the engine of our old van enters its death throes with a great clanking and scraping. It dies with abrupt finality amid beautiful pastoral countryside sadly lacking in helpful southbound lorries. Fortunately, we are within sight of a barrier post where we hire a tow into Jalalabad—by bullock cart. Sad news, we have thrown a rod through the engine block and have to hole up here until we have the engine rebuilt. By great luck there is a VW mechanic who takes Gar back into Kabul for the parts. They are more costly than we had prepared for. Lo and behold, the bank manager has been on an exchange program in Canada, understands all about bank cards and advances us the necessary cash. Three days later we have a new engine.

Days 14, 15 & 16: Jalalabad, Afghanistan

The sights are soon exhausted so we vegetate, by the last day we are quite satiated with the sights and sounds and above all, the smells of Jalalabad. It is Ramadan and meals are difficult to organize. Maushawa, pulse and yoghurt soup, stewed in mustard oil. We visit the Indian Consul to see if there would be any trouble with customs over the new engine. He assures not but it later transpires that he is wrong. But by then Gar and I have left for Canada. It cost Randy a bottle of Canadian Club to resolve the matter.

Day 17: Jalalabad, Afghanistan

Onward on the fourth day at noon. Uneventful trip and no trouble at the Pakistan border. This time we stop at the brass bazaar in Peshawar. Despite trying to be circumspect, the stall owner shouts out "Welcome, Canada, Canada diplomats." We wonder how he knows then he points out our license plate. Of course. All the stall owners' prick up their ears—such a customer means money. They all want to talk about the war situation in India and we are questioned for an hour with translators recounting our answers. We watch nervously for police. We purchase some camel saddle footstools, copper trays and tables and make our escape. We stay in Islamabad for a day and visit with members of the High Commission.

Day 18: Islamabad, Pakistan

On to Lahore. Another comfortable night at the Lahore Intercontinental but no steak dinner. This is a vegetarian day. Due to war preparations there is rationing. The soldiers have to be fed. Only Tuesdays and Thursdays are meat days. I'm afraid I do not take the news very well as I'm going back to Delhi there are no beef days. In fact, I throw a hissy fit—the poor waiter gets me my steak but cannot charge me for it.

Day 19: Lahore, Pakistan

Between the Indian and Pakistan border posts is a half a kilometre of no man's land. Easily through the Pakistan border. At the Indian border the guard demands papers. We have no papers other than the same travel papers we left with. Papers, he insists. We return to the Pakistan border to inquire about the papers they should have given us. No. No papers. Go to India. We return again to the Indian border post. After a bit of excitement, we realize he wants Pakistani newspapers to read. We have none.

We are waved through the barrier by one guard and immediately stopped by another. No explanation. Everyone's English has failed them.

We are trapped in no man's land between two countries on the brink of war. The road is a raised embankment with a short bridge ahead leading over a dry nullah, a wide deep ditch dug to allow heavy monsoon rain to run off but which quickly fills with garbage, sewage, scavenging dogs and goats, into Ferospore. We are actually on the Indian side of the border and the slope to our left is shallow and leads directly into the Ferospore bazaar. We decide to make a run for it.

The newly built engine has only one fault, it tends to backfire, loudly. And when it does people duck for cover and armed soldiers raise their guns. A potential war zone is no place for a backfiring hippie van, even a hippie van with diplomatic plates. By the time we reach Ambala our engine is backfiring so much we are afraid of being arrested so we have lunch and a tune-up.

The drive to New Delhi is uneventful.

We later learn that Indian generals were visiting the border fortifications and the guards were only trying to delay us for an hour or so until it was clear of VIPs.

Day 20: New Delhi, India

At midnight two days later, Pakistani warplanes fly a sortie over New Delhi and war is declared. The border is closed. In a surrealistic moment, from our barsati, roof patio, a group of us watch the Pakistani warplanes on their way to Agra to bomb the Taj Mahal. A while later, we watch them fly northward again. They missed. It's wrong to say that they barely interrupted our party but it was rather as though we had followed Alice down the rabbit hole.

The Day the Buddha Wept

I wrote this article after the Taliban blew up the giant Buddhas of the Bamiyan Valley but never published it. Their act still fills me with unutterable and uncomprehending sorrow.

Ottawa, March, 2001

A muffled boom, a puff of dust and they are gone. Fifteen centuries of existence ended. Despite the worldwide efforts of UNESCO, Buddhist groups, historical conservation organizations and offers to remove them, the giant Buddhas of Bamiyan are destroyed.

Two years ago not many people in North America were familiar with the place names of Afghanistan. Then a group of zealots called the Taliban gained control of the Afghan government. Suddenly, Mazar-i-Sharif, Kandahar, Herat, Balkh, Jalalabad and Kabul are in our living rooms.

It has been more than thirty years since I drove from New Delhi in India, up through the Punjab and Pakistan, through the Kyber Pass and the Kabul Gorge, through the Salang Pass and the Hindu Kush to the Oxus River, deep into the border country where Afghanistan, the Soviet Union and China meet. Those were the days of the Cold War with the USSR pointing missiles at the west and the Cultural Revolution destroying China from the inside. To look across the border was to breathe the same air as the enemy and risk looking him in the face.

The early 70's saw the last flowering of the Age of Aquarius and the overland journeys of Flower Children in painted vans to remote corners of Indian, Pakistan, Nepal and Afghanistan in search of inner knowledge and escape from the Viet Nam War. We joined the trek for inarticulate reasons of our own; two middle class couples in an old red Volkswagen van armed only with a Fodor's Guide and well intended curiosity.

In Mazar-i-Sharif we stayed in a sprawling centuries old palace cum hotel. Stripped to its bones, devoid of carpets and tapestries it revealed blue and turquoise mosaics, graceful arches, wandering corridors and empty windows offering sweeping views of the northern plateau and the distant Koh-i-Baba Mountains. The sleeping rooms had high ceilings, stone floors and were devoid of decoration except for the various hues of pink and brown in the native stone. There were no closets or dressers or drapes or mats. The only light was a kerosene lantern but the bed and linens were immaculate, modern and comfortable.

It was during this short respite that we met Rick, a wandering Canadian, who asked to join our journey. In return he offered to share his more extensive knowledge of Afghanistan. An inveterate hiker, he extolled the virtue of being at a site before sunrise so that one could gaze in solitary wonder at the glory of a technicolour dawn.

Thus, on a chilly October morning in 1971, I took a sandy seat on a hillock on the outskirts of Balkh, faced the east and waited. Almost imperceptibly, then with gathering speed the eastern sky turned pearly grey, then gold and mauve and pink and the arch of heaven spread across the land in joyous celebration of another day. A sky such as Genghis Khan, Tamerlane or Alexander the Great might have witnessed. The very hillock on which I sat was part of an ancient fortification and had felt the feet of such as they. Here the contemplative Buddhist Emperor Ashoka or the mighty Emperor Babur could have walked. Marco Polo may have passed through here on the road to Samarkand and back again to Persepolis. This was the nexus of the ancient trade routes and the gateway of conquerors. This was swimming without a life jacket in the river of history.

The local account said that this wall had been erected by Alexander the Great in the 3rd century Before the Common Era (BCE). It was a little worn, tunneled through here and there where it blocked the common way and scarred with a tracery of goat paths. It stood there as it had since it was built, no sign revealing its history, no chip van or tourist kiosk marring the landscape, a few goats and one watchful little boy were the only living things in sight.

Behind me, a few metres away, was a squat domed building decorated with an intricate pattern of blue tiles, many of which had fallen away. It was empty, unused except as casual shelter.

"Zoroaster was born here about 2500 years ago," said Rick, "Busephalous is buried over there".

Confucius, Zoroaster, Buddha, Jesus, the Prophet Mohammed— this was a landscape such as they had seen.

"Who was Busephalous?" I asked.

"Alexander the Great's favourite horse. That's his memorial," he said, pointing to the empty building. No wonder the tiles were falling off, that was 2300 years ago.

"This is wonderful. Thank you for showing it to me," I said.

"There is another place. But we would have to fly. It's four days by road and I have to leave in three."

He assumed he was coming with us.

"Where?" I asked.

"The Bamiyan Valley. It was a large Buddhist sanctuary, housing thousands of monks and contains the largest standing statues of the Buddha in the world. Hardly anyone goes there." That wasn't quite true but not many people went there.

I will never know if he did it deliberately but he had played his cards well. After a brief conference we agreed that we wanted to go and he could come with us. Balkh was the appetizer and Bamiyan would be the main course.

Bactar Airlines from Kabul to Bamiyan on a Canadian built Twin Otter in a threatening storm: ragged desolate mountain ranges, roiling black clouds sweeping in waves out of the north, Visual Flight Rules and a pilot with a hangover. Whether by skill or prayer we landed on a gravel strip with a few feet to spare. Beside us a Soviet made Yak-40 was practicing take-offs and landings preparatory to bringing in tours from Kabul—one of the remotest sites in the world and they are bringing in tours! It was a few feet longer than the Twin Otter. A critical factor as the runway sloped first down, then up, and at one point the plane had to bridge the transition without either tail or nose digging a furrow in the gravel. The runway and a storm ditch intersected at right angles. The Twin Otter, if the pilot touched the wheels down at the leading edge of the runway, could stop nose down just before the up slope began. We felt a surge of Canadian pride at the rugged capability of our little Twin Otter.

A stocky smiling man in loose black trousers, kurta, cap and Western jacket greeted us and grabbed our bed rolls and duffle bags. He flung them into an open jeep and took off over the fields toward our yurts. The bags could ride, we could walk. Tourism had arrived in Bamiyan with the filming of "The Horseman", an American made movie based on the novel by Joseph Kessels. Yurts had been built for the actors and furnished with Sears and Roebuck beds, pillows and wool blankets.

Left behind when the filming was completed, it created instant hotel accommodation where Indian, Chinese, Soviet and Western tourists could bed down in comfort. The local tourist promoter had understood rightly that being in a remote Afghan valley should not interfere with a tourist's sleep.

We were offered either horse or jeep to tour the valley sights. There was the walled village with its dusty paths, the wandering river, a few gravel roads lined with a windbreak of deciduous trees and, of course, the remnants of the Buddhist monastery and the giant Buddhas themselves. We chose to have a meander around the near valley on horseback before seeing the statues on the morrow. Not a wise choice but interesting. Hard mouthed and hard headed Mongol ponies. Wooden saddles and a rope bridle. Dinner. Bed.

Breakfast. During the twenty minute jeep ride, the shape of the statue gradually emerged from the sandstone cliff. It towered over us. Humbling, as it was meant to be. To reach the head of the tallest Buddha, we had to climb a winding path up and through the levels of abandoned caves which had served as the monks' cells.

Gautama Buddha was born in Sarnath, India, in 566 BCE. During the next five hundred years, Buddhism spread southward through Hindu India, east through Asia and Confucian China, and northward into the mountains and valleys of the Himalayas. This was the peak of its influence. During the last 25 centuries, Buddhism has established its place throughout Asia while Judaism, Christianity and Islam evolved their separate world paths from their birthplaces in the Middle East.

Sometime in the early centuries of the Common Era (CE), a large Buddhist community was established in the Bamiyan Valley. By the 20th century, all that remained was the honeycomb of caves and two giant statues, the largest 53 metres tall and the lesser, 38 metres. Hsuan-Tsang, a Chinese Buddhist priest, visited the Valley in 632 CE, a century after the statues were built and the same year in which the Prophet Mohammed died in Medina. Hsuan-Tsang wrote that there were ten monasteries, a thousand priests, 20 thousand cave dwellings and that the face of the giant Buddha was covered with gold and decorated with precious gems "that dazzle the eye". Reports from the 10th century tell of a still thriving community. In 1222, Genghis Khan, in a rage over the death of his grandson, defaced the statues and slaughtered the remaining population of the valley, ending Buddhist influence in Afghanistan which today is primarily Muslim. By the 13th century, it is quite probable that the population was already severely reduced.

By 1971, a thousand people lived in the Valley. The statues had become faceless and limbless, their painted garments and surrounding frescoes obliterated. Unpainted and undecorated, their impressive presence remained ensured by the dignity of age and their awesome size. The face of the taller Buddha was featureless from brow to upper lip as though a great knife had sliced off its eyes and nose. Hands and legs had been amputated. However, for whatever reason, the lips and chin remained and the Buddha seemed to be calmly smiling still.

The Bamiyan Valley is 3500 metres above sea level and the climb to the top of the statue another 300. I was gasping and clinging to the walls by the time I reached the archway to the flat crown of Buddha's head. The last of the path is inside the mountain and nearly pitch dark. The abrupt transition into the brilliant sunlight onto a carpet sized platform, 60 metres above the valley floor with no railing, was startling and I staggered under the vision. There was room to sit down and I did so. The lotus position is perfectly acceptable for viewing the world from Buddha's head.

"Come to me in silence" advised the Buddha. I did.

Silent except for the soughing of the wind, the schussing of the sand, and the beating of my heart. The brown walled village, the reddish fallow fields, the little black dots of goats, the turquoise river, the golden leaved windbreaks, the pink sand of the arid plain and the perpetually snow capped Koh-i-Baba mountains. Autumn in Bamiyan. How many eyes had gazed over the same scene? How many meditations inspired? How many prayers offered?

Islam arrived and the statues survived. The Mongol hordes came and the statues survived, albeit, their faces did not. The monks left and the statues survived. The Soviets used them for target practice and they survived. A wonder from the ancient world, isolated in their valley, visited by a few tourists and photographers, they existed only on the margins of 21st century concern.

Until the Taliban. In a passion of ideological fervor, the Taliban decided to destroy these singular monuments. They declared the giant

Buddha statues of the Bamiyan Valley to be an affront to Islam and an abomination to be erased. And erase them they did. With dynamite.

These statues were wonders from antiquity, ancient symbols of a philosophy not practiced in the region for 1400 years. A philosophy which in 25 centuries has never declared a religious crusade nor forced anyone to accept their ways. In destroying them, the Taliban demonstrated beyond doubt that there would be no dialogue, no negotiations with their regime.

The Dalai Lama said, "Hatreds do not cease in this world by hating, but by not hating; this is an eternal truth."

I am trying.

The Seeker

Under this sky and heaven
I am here in this moment.
Along the way my feet have trod
Silent companions in a search
For answers to questions
Timeless when dawn broke on human awareness.

Who am I?
Who are you?
Why are we here?

I seek answers in God's cathedrals
But the prayers fade in the
Glory of the light cascading through
Stained glass windows
And the feel of the stone worn hollow
Under my feet on the sanctuary stairs.

If I could find the essential question
I could seek the answer.
My question burns but has no form.

What is my purpose?
Why was I born?
Are we part of a plan?
Whose plan?

On the silent marble of an ancient mosque
I kneel and touch my head
To the stone cold floor;
The shadows and light through the carved
Jalousies weave intricate designs
And distract me from my searching;

My toes relish the smooth tile and cool relief
From the burning sand
Of the scorching marketplace
Through which I came.
I lose myself in the beauty of simple line and sunlight.

Purple mountain fingers scratch the belly
Of a passionless sky.
Wind snaps the prayer cloths
Strung like signal flags from rocky cairns
Along the treeless Tibetan pass
Shaking the prayers free
And whispering them in Buddha's ear.
A pilgrim claps his hands
And shouts to attract attention to his plea.
The towering peaks stretch endless on forever.
The clouds lie at my feet.
No eagle soars, no flower blooms,
Only the wind, the light and the mountains.
No man made this,
No man can live here,
Surely this is the home of gods.
Lost to the awesome majesty and numbing cold,
I forget to ask my question.

I forget my question.

Rose and sandalwood,
Coconut and mango, wood smoke
And urine, the scents of an ageless shrine
Cling to my nostrils.
The importuning of beggars and vendors,
The chink and chime of temple bells,
The bellow of a sacred cow,
The sounds of a thousand, five thousand, years.
Barefoot I feel my way down,
Down the blackened stairs

Grimed with the smoke of a million oil lamps,
Worn with the tread of a billion humble feet,
To offer a gift of flowers and rice in return for
Protection from the calamities of life—
And insight, a glimmer in the darkness of ignorance.
In the flickering glow of three thousand years
Of worship my questioning shrivels to impertinence.
I dare not ask for enlightenment.

I yield.
Under this sky and heaven
My purpose is here in this moment.
I must accept the unknown.
In matters of faith
There is no Quad Erat Demonstratum.

Reassigned

New Delhi, June, 1772

We are going home. The sea lift is packed and has been hauled away on a bullock cart and our air freight delivered to the airport. Only our suitcases remain. The past three years have been indescribable: a sensory experience of tastes, sights, sounds and smells; an intellectual challenge to cultural and religious paradigms; an opportunity beyond my ability to exploit. People ask "What is India like?" My trite answer is, "Say what you like, it is all true."

India is beautiful and ugly, ancient and modern, spiritual and venal, inspiring and disgusting. Days I love it and others I hate it. I love it but I could not live here. I do not belong and, no matter how long I stayed, I would never belong. I feel one has to be born here to even begin to develop any understanding of the complexity of the Indian culture. It is old. Old beyond the grasp of someone from the west. Old and layered and subtle and phantasmagorical. This on top of the fact that this was our first posting overseas. Without a briefing or leaflet of information the family of young officers are sent abroad to cope with local language, culture, shopping and housing and schools and diplomatic hospitality. Sink or swim, it's up to you.

We arrived in July, most personnel were away on home leave, others had been transferred and not replaced, the bachelors were no help to a family and within six weeks I had been at post longer than most. I was trying to help the newcomers! Complaint? No. It was make or break and I intended not to break. The list of what I did not know was endless. It was lucky that I did not understand how much I did not understand.

Take the fact that Indian households are managed with servants, any or all of the following: bearer, cook, houseboy(s), nanny, driver, sweeper, laundryman, gardener, watchman and assorted itinerant regulars who come to the door to deliver the day's milk or vegetables, to collect the garbage, to provide haircuts, shaves, massages or dressmaking. Who knew? I did understand about the nanny or *ayah*, she was a priority if I was to cope at all with diplomatic life. It was a disaster at first and I apologize to those I practiced on and then fired—it was my incompetence not theirs.

Take shopping. To keep control over household spending I decided to continue to do the shopping myself. This meant local markets, mainly Khan Market, a collection of permanent stalls around a grassy square that sells vegetables, fruit, chicken and a small store that sells soap, milk powder and an assortment of national tinned products. Don't think Canadian products, these are not cook from scratch substitutes. All our meals are produced from scratch: tomato soup from tomatoes, bread from soft wheat flour, milk that comes from water buffalos and pasteurized in our kitchen, no salads or uncooked food of any kind, scratch cakes and cookies. We boil all our water, even our infant son's bath water until he became old enough to be trusted not to drink it. If the boys need a shirt, we have it made. If I need a new dress, an old one is picked apart and used as a pattern. Ground spices are wrapped in newspaper cones, vegetables go into cloth bags which I bring to the market. Fish is bought at the fish market; lamb and buffalo at the Muslim market; pork at the Hindu market. I bring my own ice buckets to carry it home. Each visit I run a gamut of little boys who want to watch the car, carry my bags, send me to their uncle's shop. The ground is littered with garbage being swept up by raggedy women. The low stucco walls are topped with rows of men perched on their haunches, smoking bedis and eying my every move.

Young policemen stand about in their uniforms, carrying bamboo lathis. Their eyes are alert. A swiftly welded lathi can break a bone or remove an eye. Everyone keeps their peace.

Some of the foreign women come to the market in their tennis whites; the men and policemen alike admire the view of exposed white leg flesh, a sight never revealed by their own women.

The handiest household tips actually came from my grandmother who always washed the tins before opening them, who always stored her flour and sugar and salt in sealed containers, who assumed a mouse or two was going to get in and kept house accordingly, and who waged war on flies and mosquitoes like a storm trooper. The other sources of practical information are the British women. They have been here a long time and have learned to accommodate the heat, pests and monsoon rains. I have learned to avoid advice from foreigners who are paid too much and do not have to live on the local market.

Not that I am limited to the local market in every way. We have our own little commissary that we share with the Australians and recently we have been admitted to the American commissary. My first visit there was a cultural experience. By then I had been in India for two years and isolated from western ways. The women wore tight little polyester shorts and had pink plastic curlers in their hair. I had forgotten all about those. They were fussing about the lack of taco sauce and Rice Crispies. I had not seen bread flour, white salt, tomato ketchup or peanut butter in months. Taco sauce seemed irrelevant in a shop that sold toilet paper, tomato soup and strawberry jam. The field day ended when I began checking prices. My kitchen had gone two years without most of these things and could continue to do so for another year. I did buy flour and peanut butter—Indian maida does not make good bread nor does peanut butter from ground raw peanuts make good peanut butter.

This last year the Canadian government has built a compound and a new Canadian High Commission building in Chanakapuri, a designated diplomatic enclave. To my mind, living on the compound would be too easy. Why join the Gymkhana Club if you have your own swimming pool? Why learn how an Indian family lives if you can shop at the commissary? It would be easier. It takes a little incentive to step out into a country so vast and different from our own. But how much you would miss.

Our children are too young for regular school. They attend Safdarjung Playschool along with both Indian and foreign children, granted, the Indian children are from wealthy families. Their ayah goes with them and she stays with the youngest, who is three at this point, for the morning. If he gets tired, she takes him aside for a nap under a shade tree. So do the other children, there are as many ayahs as children. Very civilized and very comforting for the children.

Throughout the year we celebrate national, Christian, Hindu and Muslim holidays. In fact, every month has a celebration of some kind, sometimes more. We hang lights for Diwali as well as Christmas. At Christmas we hang them on shrubs or even banana trees, for Diwali we drape them over the balcony wall. At Holi we give out sweets and toss coloured powder. We do not fast for Ramadan but we celebrate the end of the season at a feast with our neighbour. At Christmastime some of the shopkeepers put a little artificial tree next to their puja shrine to

Humayun. India is a land of spirituality and religion: Hinduism, Islam, Christianity, Sikhism, Buddhism, Jainism, Zoroastrianism, Judaism are all practiced although Hinduism is the overwhelming majority. At a political level there is tension but at the neighbourhood level there is frequently respect and friendship although not intermarriage. They all welcome secular foreigners and it is an unparalleled opportunity for spiritual growth.

The music. At first grating, atonal and unphrased, nasal and unintelligible. Gradually, I learned to appreciate the repeating patterns of ragas, a seven note "scale" without harmonies or chords but with melodies and rhythms.

The painting. Detailed and full of mythical meaning, executed without European techniques to relay three dimensions. Scenes float above, below and around each other without regard for perspective. It takes repeated exposure to appreciate their beauty.

The dance. Exotic and colourful, the intricate foot movements, the angularity of the arms and shoulders, the grace of the hands and the expression of the eyes. Inseparable from the music and religious devotion. Total contrast to classical ballet.

Indians are family centred and their families are large and extended, even a family celebration includes dozens, sometimes hundreds, of people. They love a celebration and celebrate at all their festivals and holidays. Diplomatic life includes many of these occasions as well as purely inter-mission ones. Consequently, we are out most evenings, some weeks it is every night and often it is several events in one night. We distinguish between official events, or representational occasions which we refer to as "functions", and non-official ones. Official representation costs are offset to an extent by allowances from the Department for food and clothing. This determination is made by whether the occasion furthers the aims of the mission as outlined by guidelines established in Ottawa. Difficult to tell sometimes so one relies on professional judgment. Most occasions can be turned to advantage if they are "worked" properly. That usually means, how many local contacts one makes as versus how much time one spends chatting with friends. At any gathering there is always someone who knows someone you've been trying to see. The social contact or introduction is a necessary first step to access, another important duty of a diplomat. A diplomat with access to people with information or power or authority is more valuable than one without.

There are several concepts here that differ dramatically from the Canadian norm: privacy, gratitude and community responsibility. Privacy does not exist as I understand it because personal space does not exist. It is too crowded, the house is full of servants and wanting to be alone is strange and suspicious. Having marital relations interrupted by the bearer bringing morning tea is normal household routine. He does his duty and sahib does his. Oh, yeah?

There is no obligation on the part of a receiver to be grateful for your generosity. You are lucky to be in a position to give, it is your duty to give and all merit goes to you anyway. Why should the recipient be grateful? He is doing his part by being there to give to. That is his karmic duty and if he fulfils it he may be the giver in the next life. I once gave our gardener a practically new jacket that had belonged to my father. He sold it. What? Once I gave it, it was his. The money was more useful and allowed him to feed his family, or pay school fees, or buy boots or whatever. Attitude adjust, Memsahib.

The definition of community, the part for which you are responsible, is more narrowly defined. There is a very small volunteer sector in India spearheaded by followers of Gandhi, Mother Teresa and overseas volunteer organizations. The one I got to know is Crèches of India which supports a safe area for the children of workers at construction sites. Women do most of the fetch and carry at building sites. Their children come with them and live and play on the site and they were doing so at the site of the new Canadian High Commission. The Crèches organization erected a roofed concrete slab with a small store room as a shelter and provided early schooling, meals, supervision and first aid to children from birth to 12 years. I volunteer there. Mother Teresa provides care and shelter for people of the streets. However, usually, people do not volunteer for the general good of society. They accept responsibility for family, extended family, family retainers and assist selected needy who habituate the mosque or temple where they pray. There are too many people in need.

There are needy people everywhere. And they are in your face everywhere. Old beggars. Child beggars. Sadhus. Crippled beggars. Real beggars. Phony beggars. One is overwhelmed by the need of the poor people in India. Poverty on the streets in Ottawa does not match the need of the street people of India. There are no Missions, no Salvation Army outreach, no charities, no municipal housing, no unemployment insurance, no welfare benefits, no medical scheme, no government handouts. All depends on the charity of individuals to individuals. How can this work?

Strangely, it does, probably as successfully as charity does at home. If you are better off than someone else, you "adopt" a needier person. All other importuning you ignore. The adoption may include money, cast offs, handouts of food or things for resale. You do not accept responsibility for their decisions; you do not take on their community. You decide what you can give and that is an end to it. Once your donation level is established within their community that is, for the most part, the end of their beseeching at your door. That is not the end of the public begging that may plague your every step in the market but even there you can adopt a special one and confine your generosity.

There is too much need. Accepting what you can and cannot do is essential to survival, your survival. The bullock driver who painfully twists his animal's tail to make the scrawny beast go faster has to choose between his animal and his children. The need adjusts his concept of cruelty.

It is not your country, you will never understand it. Canada is. Charity begins at home.

KENYA : 1975-1978

We stayed three years in India before returning home to Ottawa. The children were in early elementary school, my mother was elderly with failing health and living with my sister, we needed to buy a house; it was time to go home and so we did.

Three years later and it was time to pack up again. This time to Kenya, East Africa. Luck does play a role. Our shipments had been packed and labeled for Beirut, Lebanon, but looming war threatened to became actual war and we headed for Africa. Just as well, six weeks later, Beirut blew up and we would have had to return home. As it turned out, this was a perfect time to be in Kenya.

At this time, Njomo Kenyatta had been President of Kenya for twelve years, since independence in 1963. The country was doing modestly well with tourism, coffee, tea and ivory. Roads were paved; schools were available through grade five for boys, three for girls, for the price of the uniforms; national parks gave the illusion of environmental conscience and democratic elections of democracy. Kenya was an African showpiece, a country of peace and rationality where racism and tribalism just might give way to reason.

This was in contrast to Uganda where President Idi Admin ruled in dictatorial cruelty; where fear and poverty pervaded; where shops were empty, schools and hospitals closed; where people disappeared and children starved to death.

The Canadian High Commission in Nairobi was also responsible for Uganda and for the Canadians who wound up in trouble there. And across that border, trouble was not hard to find.

Whether it was Canadian priests, nuns, doctors, journalists; whether it was their fault or not, they were arrested regularly and in need of any assistance Canada could provide. By Canada that meant my husband or another mid-level diplomat would have to take the Land Rover loaded with petrol for the journey, gifts for Ugandan officials and, protected only by the colour and script of a passport, travel up country and see what, if anything, could be done. The colour of the passport was important because most of the border guards and police could not read the script. One hoped they remembered that the red cover indicated someone who should not be arrested or shot on sight.

Kenya, in contrast, offered relative safety except from the car thieves, house burglars, police, drivers of cars, trucks, private taxis and pickpockets. Of course, there was always the problem of being in the wrong place at the wrong time. The death penalty was handed out for burglary and theft whether or not the robber shot the victim, so shooting the innocent driver or the homeowner was common. My greatest fear was whether or not they would allow me to grab my children out of the back seat before they took off with my car.

The only motto to live by was "be circumspect and enjoy the Kenyan lifestyle". Safari and party but prepare your emergency plans whether for civil unrest or earthquake.

Kenyan Kaleidoscope

Nairobi, Kenya, 1975

Ivory and slave traders. Tarzan. Stephanie Powers and William Holden. Lions, elephants and wildebeests. Safari country. These are media-generated images. Within a few days one discovers that this only hints at the diversity of history, life, topography and ethnography to explore, both intellectually and physically. From paleoanthropology to bird watching, photography to mountain climbing, desert to alpine meadow, Hilton Hotel to canvas tent, for the spectator or the sportsman, for the novice or the expert, Kenya offers a gourmet's palette of things to see and do and learn. When the East African Community had been functioning, one could travel at will throughout Kenya, Tanzania and Uganda. However, politics alters reality and now one must approach each country separately. Visitors to Tanzania must fly in to Dar-es-Salaam from outside Kenya, and visitors to Uganda are nearly always on some business of their own, not a tourist's pleasure.

The single most significant event in the emergence of modern Kenya was the decision of the British government to build a railway from Mombasa on the Indian Ocean to Port Florence, now called Kisumu, on Lake Victoria. This incredible engineering feat through desert and lion-infested, fever-plagued scrub country, across volcanic ridges and quagmire took from 1895 to 1901. The railroad eased colonization and the establishment of a colonial government; turned a highland swamp into the city of Nairobi; cut across traditional migration paths of people and wildlife; encouraged settlement along this corridor which facilitated the spread of education, religious teaching and smallpox; accelerated the competition between agricultural land and wildlife range; introduced a large population of Asians, recruited from India as workers and traders, and provided reliable, rapid transportation of goods and services.

Equipped with handbooks identifying flora and fauna, armed with historical facts from dipping judiciously into *Zamani* by B.A. Ogot, and stimulated by the insights and tales of *The Lunatic Express* by Charles Miller, one can take the train from Mombasa to the Lake Victoria port of Kisumu while reliving a century of East African history and development. The train provides a leisurely opportunity to view the flowers, trees, bird and animal life; see Kenyans, black, white and Asian living in traditional, transitional and contemporary style; and rest, read, dine and take photographs en route.

The coast with its heat and humidity, its strong Arabic influence in architecture and facial features, its sweet pawpaws, cashew nuts and fresh fish provides an exotic background for a tropical vacation. Although the drive from the coast to Nairobi takes only five hours, the train provides an interesting, if slower, alternative. One can board in Mombasa after tea, settle the children and suitcases, change clothes and repair to the dining car for a leisurely five course dinner impeccably served on fine china with silver service, heavy linen tablecloths, fine wines and the world's best coffee. The gleam of darkly polished wood, burgundy carpeting, white-jacketed waiters and dim lighting create a protective cocoon that is hardly disturbed by the swaying of the two straining locomotives as they begin their 14-hour, 510-km. climb to Nairobi.

By the time darkness makes its dramatic equatorial entrance, the train has left the coastal plain with its lush vegetation, fringing coral reef and clustered villages and entered the Athi Plains — a dry, red dusty desert with sparse clumps of elephant grass, conical termite mounds, fleshy baobab trees and scattered gatherings of acacia trees.

Through here one can still find the vast, though dwindling, herds of elephant and antelope with their omnipresent predators and see the Masai people with their herds of cattle, bead decorations and beer-can earrings. This is a harsh region and cannot support any great density of life. It created a barrier to inland travel with the exception of ivory and slave caravans, and accounts for the readily visible differences between coastal tribes and those further inland. The coastal tribes show the results of centuries of Arabic influence in language, facial features, architecture, decorative design and religion, whereas the inland tribes have adapted influences from the successive waves of migrations from the central and Nilotic regions of Africa.

Gradually the desert landscape becomes savannah and then scrub, a few hills appear and the train begins the steeper climb into the Kenyan highlands and Nairobi, a modern city 1,677 m. above sea level.

Nairobi is a visitor's delight with familiar hotels and gift shops for the timid, native style markets and colonial style inns for the more hardy. Here Pierre Cardin suits walk side by side with goat skin capes;

bold printed cotton wraps called kangas mingle with polyester slacks; linen safari suits custom tailored in New York or London share the dusty tourist van with faded cotton ready-mades. Nairobi is the economic, political and tourist heart of Kenya. This is where most international flights first land, where the railway branches north, where the highway puts forth its tarmac spokes, where the parliament sits, where the diplomatic community lives and where the poor and out-of-work come for succour. Here one can still sit à la Hemingway at the Long Bar at the (New) Stanley Hotel, or eat curry on the veranda of the Norfolk Hotel as did the early settlers. Nairobi is surrounded by small farms and large coffee estates. Coffee is second only to tourism in earning Kenya needed foreign currency. The laterite soil, specific altitude, hot days and cool nights allow Kenya to grow the Arabica coffee bean prized for flavour and which, when blended with the less demanding Robusta bean, produces what most of us drink.

Remember Elspeth Huxley's *Flame Trees of Thika*? The village of Thika lies 45 km. to the north. The road follows the same ox cart trail and one can still take tea at the Blue Post Inn. Here, too, is Fourteen Falls where Tarzan first swung in pectoral splendor. Remember Elsa, Joy Adamson's lion friend? Travel another 250 km. to Meru Game Reserve and you can sit on Elsa's Rock. Here rises 5,085-m. high Mt. Kenya from whose various tribal names comes the country's name. Travel another 600 km. through the arid, dangerous terrain of the Chalbi Desert, salt pan remains of an ancient sea, and, one arrives on the shores of Lake Turkana. Here fishing expeditions seek the enormous Nile perch which, while considerably less than trophy size, still makes a delicious dinner for 50. It is on the northeast shore of this lake that Richard Leakey found the hominid fossils which possibly date back 1.2 to 2.3 million years and add fuel to the prehistory debate.

Trains making up in Nairobi for the continuing journey to Lake Victoria often put on three locomotives to ensure sufficient power to haul and control the cars as they first climb to the edge of the Great Rift Valley before descending the eastern escarpment, then climb again to the highest point of the railroad and descend to Kisumu. Skirting Lake Naivasha which offers camp grounds, fishing, swimming and an English Sunday brunch and passing through Nakuru where hundreds of thousands of flamingos, pelicans and storks make their home at the bird sanctuary, the train creeps up the western escarpment to the Mau Summit which rises 2,535 m. above sea level.

Although this is too far north to see them, directly south are the vast grasslands of south-west Kenya and north-west Tanzania that are home to the enormous herds of wildebeests, Cape buffalo and elephant so often filmed as background for the mellifluous voices of Lorne Greene or Richard Attenborough. At the edge of these migration routes, along the banks of a long dry river bed, is a prehistoric site containing hand-axe heads, carefully crafted by Acheulian hunter-gatherers between 100,000 and 500,000 years ago.

At this height the land is lush and ripe for the production of tea which likes to be cooler, higher and better nourished than coffee. The pickers work in groups, identified by the bright colour of their smocks as to which team they belong. The smocks are made of oilskin so that the women can slide easily through the closely planted bushes without bruising the leaves. From Kericho to Kisumu the countryside changes. It is more productive with more farms and fewer gardens planted tight to the edge of the tarmac. This is upcountry Kenya — tea estates, fruit farms, sheep and cattle ranches — where even the facial features of the people are different for different influences affected the development in this region for thousands of years. These people are tribally closer to the Nilotic peoples of Uganda than to the Bantu-descended peoples of the highlands around Nairobi, and both are different from the coastal peoples. Here grow the world's most succulent avocados. No crab stuffing is needed to make a meal of these brutes. A few drops of Lea and Perrins, or a wedge of lime, turn one into a feast.

Lake Victoria, second largest body of fresh water in the world, is so large that Kenya has two coasts—one salt water, the other fresh—and the breezes off both are a welcome relief to the traveler. Mombasa to Kisumu has taken 36 hours while the track climbed and dropped a total of 4,863 m., and covered 936 km.

Few tourists bother to come this far west now that Uganda is off the itinerary which is unfortunate since it is seeing western Kenya that allows one to appreciate its astounding diversity. However, Idi Amin rules in Uganda and his police, secret police, military units and body guards run everything with implacable corrupt authority. Gone are the lush plantations of coffee, sugar and cocoa, gone are the thriving small farms and abundant produce, gone are the middle class and the intellectual class, gone are the huge herds of wild game, gone are the tourists who came to see them, gone are the days when Uganda had the possibility to feed east Africa. Anyone who could has gone and those left live in poverty and fear.

Kenya has cut communication with Tanzania because of its looser stand on South African apartheid, Kenya had cut ties with Uganda because of its leader's unpredictability and so, the East African Community has disintegrated and its former members are going it alone.

Haven't We Met Before?

Nairobi, Kenya, 1975

"Oh, Lord," I pray, "give me the strength to do it all again."

After the hassle of managing yet another household move, the fatigue of long distance travel and the pain of parting from elderly family, it does not seem fair that I now have to integrate myself into still another unfamiliar milieu.

"Some things are gonna be, Laurie Ann," my father used to say, "no sense in workin' up a lather."

With that succinct advice in my mind, I had accepted the invitation to a Buffet Bash extended by a Fellow Canadian at the mission. "Really casual," he had said. "Give you a chance to meet some of the Canadians before the official round of parties starts."

Actually, he lied. The party was full of casual official people.

"Official parties". I recall them from the last posting, the endless line of unfamiliar faces and foreign names, the struggle with a recently learned language and the conflict with the needs of my children. In this case I only learned enough Swahili for travelling about the country. The lingua franca is English although the Kenyan accent is confusing to me.

The tinkle of ice on glass and the buzz of cocktail chatter swirl through the mist of the Vapo-mat Mosquito Zapper as my feet struggle for a foothold on the slippery terrazzo stairs. Why do people wax terrazzo stairs? Blast new shoes and leather soles. I mutter the litany to myself, "the expatriate community is a source of friends, the expatriate community is a source of information, the expatriate community needs you, therefore, circulate."

"Into the breach," I think, unclasping my husband's arm and preparing to play 'Red Rover, Come Over' with the crush of people in the sunken living room. It is a constant in diplomatic life, graciously leaving communities of familiar people and smoothly entering one of strangers. It is unavoidable that we become rather like chameleons, changing character and colour to blend in while we assess the situation.

"...Fred and Alice," "...like you to meet," "know you will..."

"...so pleased," "... love it." I smile and burble frenetically while my mind pairs names and faces—beard with glasses equals Stan, beard without glasses equals married to Sarah.

Then, as I grip the limp hand of Miss Low-Cut Red-Dress and elude the beery buss of Mr. Green Shirt, a familiar voice catches a thermal and lands in my ear.

"...recommend it, it's just like home."

Ah, yes, it is Mr. Maple Leaf. I spot him in the corner by the stereo system. With rye in hand and securely surrounded by other expats, he is firmly upholding the Canadian way. He will be a sympathetic companion during bouts of homesickness.

"Have you decided whether to join the Women's Round Table yet? We're looking for someone to take over the 'Christmas for Kids' fund raising."

Mrs. Bustling Beaver holds my elbow and gives me her don't-let-the-side-down look. I had arrived a mere twenty-four hours previously, still I hesitate to admit that I had never heard of the Round Table. I assure her that once I am slightly more settled, I will talk to her but, regrettably, this time I must refuse—the children to settle into school, you know. God bless them, always an unassailable excuse, the children.

I ease past the Tête-à-tête Twins staring in to each other's eyes while jabbering simultaneously and perch on the arm of a sofa. An impeccably manicured hand languidly lifts from the beige cushions and offers itself.

"Welcome to Wonderland. I hope you golf. Let me know what days you have free next week so I can plan a little luncheon. By the way, I'm Krystle Sterling."

"Hello, thank you and yes, I do," I answer, "although I rarely break 100. Thursday would be fine."

I neglect to mention that my score refers to the front nine only; time enough to clarify that when the situation arises. I want to start the posting with some credibility.

"I don't expect anyone introduced you," Krystle goes on. "It seems to be a free-for-all these days. You know, they actually pay someone to meet you at the plane now. In the old days we looked for each other for nothing. I wish I had a dollar..."

I confess that formal introductions to the gathering had been omitted but we had been met by an admin officer at the airport, assured him we were fine and could take a taxi to the hotel on our own. In reality, that is our way, to do things on our own even it though it sometimes upsets the "higher ups". In fact, the same admin officer who met us at the airport became very annoyed with us a few days later when he came to the hotel to take us out to view our assigned quarters. We had checked out and were already living in our SQ, with staff in place and our air shipment unpacked. The department only grants one a set number of days in a hotel per round trip move and we want them for our return trip to Ottawa. As to how we had located it, we had the address, pictures of the place and our crates were in the garage. We did check with the most important person—the houseman—and, thanks to the servant grapevine, he already knew our names and that we had arrived. And so, we moved in.

In rapid succession I meet Ernest Intellectual, Clever Crafter and Vanna Vague.

"Are you going to work or are you a stay at home mother?" demands Independent Erma. I wondered whether she is just curious or being defensive of a restricted job market. "What do you do?" she queries, probably hoping that I am not a job market competitor.

I find that I hate that question as much here as I do at home. Like many wives of my age and experience, I work when I have the opportunity but spend most of my time looking after my family. I prefer to think of it as a matter of choice rather than a lack of ambition or ability. Being wife and mother in a rotational family is not an opportune stage from which to launch a career; moving country to country every two or three years does not impress employers. Anyway, my field of expertise is largely indefinable. I have several degrees, some experience at teaching and a bit of writing under my belt. Nothing that would let me finish the sentence, "I am a …"

"It's too soon to know," I answer. "Perhaps I'll find that I enjoy my leisure."

I wasn't going to get into what I do, or not do; not to mention that I was too jetlagged to create an instant interesting history.

In any event, before that situation could develop, Mother Canada swoops down and herds me off to the buffet table. Being a skilled person with years of experience, in no time at all she has extracted the pertinent facts; this is my second posting, I like bird-watching and want to write books, my sons are going to attend the local American school and our dog is en route, my gall bladder is out and my ovaries in, I like fish and am allergic to nothing—"that's an asset," she comments. "People are getting more and more difficult to feed."

Satisfied with her work, she steers me to a padded chair where I recover in stunned reverence. I feel as though I have given blood. I start to nibble at the warm rice salad and frantically try to recall what inner most secrets I have gaily revealed. Was she good!

A glimmer at the edge of my sight rouses me from my reverie. Can it be? Yes, it is Beau Butterfly. Where is…? Yes, there is Belle. Momentarily at rest, clinging to the banister and sipping bubbly, they are gathering strength for their next sortie. I watch them, waiting for them to lead me on a whirlwind tour of the rich, the famous and the powerful. Within ten minutes they have patted arms, air kissed, smiled at and hand held a probable ambassador, a government minister, a senior clergyman and several of the handsomest and the richest guests in the room. Tomorrow I would invite Mother Canada to coffee and get the low down.

I sigh in relief. The gang is complete and, even though I do not know their names, they are not strangers after all. Within a few months I will know these people and we would become the close community with whom I would share the next three years. Perhaps one, if I'm lucky, might become a lifelong friend.

The Day that the Rains Came Down

Nairobi, Kenya, 1975

As usual, Ottawa officials had all scheduled their visits to sunny climes to coincide with the impending Canadian winter. We had had, in succession, an inspection team, a group of MPs, the Secretary of State for External Affairs and now, at the tag end of the visitor season, the leader of the opposition.

The High Commissioner had, with experienced foresight, arranged to be at a conference in Europe during this period and would not be available; however, his staff would extend all necessary services and hospitality. One needs to understand that politicians do not travel alone. They require an entourage of handlers to assure that all is anticipated and the unanticipated is not newsworthy. While the leader himself would be entertained by the acting head of mission, it falls to me to oversee the appropriate hospitality for the entourage. Naturally, it transpires that one evening I am simultaneously hosting a function and attending a round of cocktails with the leader which necessitates leaving my houseman, Samuel, in charge of the final arrangements for dinner.

"You not worry, Memsahib," Samuel reassures me. "When you come, dinner be ready."

A frisson of things remembered the last time he reassured me of the same thing patters down my spine, like the time he forgot the washing machine which had a hissy fit and washed my clothes for four hours. Not only Bobby Burns knew about the best-laid plans of mice and men, or, in this case, memsahibs who had to leave their houseman in charge of arrangements. Instead of reassuring me, Samuel's words have reminded me that it is not what we anticipate that creates trouble but what we do not.

As I survey the immaculate linen and sparkling crystal, the memory of jellied salad rings collapsing and sliding off their plates onto terrazzo floors and potato salads made and served with raw potatoes flashes before my eyes.

I remember the occasion when I had believed my husband's assurances that none of the Indians coming to lunch were vegetarian. To a man they had blanched and stopped chewing when I calmly assured them that the dish contained not dried beans but small shrimp. To spit or swallow, that was the question. I had heard later that the ceremonies to appease their sullied spirits took all weekend.

Then there was the time two amorous house geckos set up housekeeping in my mulberry Kirsch compote only to be discovered when the silver lid was lifted and Frau Kleine was sipping her tea. Her English and her composure had fled simultaneously. The tea stains never did come out of the table cloth.

I sigh. The current hot weather heralds the onset of the long rains and there is little I could do about the heat but everything else seems to be under control. It is significant that this will be my first rainy season in Kenya.

"Rain tonight," comments Samuel. "I close the windows?" he queries.

I wonder why he should ask such a thing when it is obvious that closed windows will only make the sweltering house even hotter.

"No," I instruct and leave to attend the early reception.

Oh, foolish me.

When I dash into the residence three hours later, five minutes ahead of the entourage and assorted Excellencies and Honourables, I find the house staff, the gardener, their wives and children frenetically sweeping tables, chairs, floors and window sills with makeshift brooms and dustpans.

"What are you doing?" I cry.

"It rained, Memsahib."

"Yes, I know."

Not even babes in the womb could have missed the roof-denting downpour. However, I had missed something—two things, in fact. Firstly, I had forgotten to follow the instruction to leave the windows open with the instruction to close them if it rained. Secondly, I forgot about the termites.

Stimulated by the first of the rains, East African termite ants leave their underground tunnels and take to the air in prenuptial flight. They swarm in their millions, then shed their gossamer wings and fall to earth to mate. My dining-room had become a gigantic wedding palace. It looked like a miniature pink sausage factory gone mad.

"I close the windows now, Memsahib?" asks Samuel.

"Yes," I confirm in a calm "I'm completely relaxed about this" voice. "Close the windows, and make sure there are no termites in the wine glasses."

The gleeful gleam in his eyes confirms that this had all transpired as he had known it would. His greenhorn memsahib had had no idea of the impact that rain had on broody termites, and, he had covered himself by having informed me that it would rain this evening and ensuring that I wanted the windows open.

As I go off to serve a delaying round of drinks, Samuel assures me, "You no worry, Memsahib. When you come, dinner be ready."

As I leave the room, I tip a wriggling, dying termite out of a wine glass onto the floor and squash it under foot.

"Clean that up, please," I instruct, reasserting my authority and leaving the field with tattered dignity.

True to his word, all was clean and ordered fifteen minutes later as we enter the dining room in diplomatic pomp and hierarchy. Dinner is delicious with no added pieces of protein that I can spy.

I wonder if the guests have noticed anything untoward in the evening's meal. "No", I think, "diplomats could have carried it off no matter what they spied but politicians, no, they are not that good at covering up." Actually, they are but a wiggling termite in their curry might have been too much.

Next morning, cook assures me that the queen termite is delicious when fried and extremely healthful, a delicacy kept for the boys and men of the family. My boys reject his offer of a crispy fried golden yellow two inch egg sack despite his assurances of its savour.

So begins a two year battle with post administration to fit all the windows with screens. I lose. They sell the house and we move into new quarters, with screens.

Paradise Under Seige

Kampala, Uganda, 1976

In the 1970's, Uganda is shaped by the stupidity, greed and egotistical cunning of its President for Life, Idi Amin. Canada still has diplomatic relations with Uganda which are safely carried out from Nairobi in adjacent Kenya, however, it is sometimes necessary to actually go there and make an effort to retain enough credibility to care for our remaining nationals who run hospitals and schools there. We are on our way to Gulu and Masaka, a circuitous route to Kampala, the capitol.

The explosive bang ricochets around the inside of the white Peugeot station wagon. We hit the floor; the driver hits the gas pedal and the car races down the disintegrating highway, ignoring potholes and sunbathing monkeys alike. This is Idi Amin's Uganda and loud noises are not something to safely linger about investigating.

The border with Kenya is several hours behind us. There are no villages, no people walking along the road and no other vehicles, not even military traffic. Highway maintenance has been neglected for so long that the vegetation grows lushly to the edge of the pavement and even in the cracks and holes. The unspoken anxiety of running afoul of local military or police lurks in everyone's mind.

In this case, the momentary panic has been caused by a bottle of soda water popping its top. In addition to all our own gear, we carry cooking oil, soap, kerosene, salt and flour to leave with the Canadians we will visit during our tour.

There are only a few Canadians left in Uganda in 1976, mostly White Fathers parish priests, White Sisters nurses, and Brothers of Christian Instruction teachers. Most of them live in the southwest around Mbarara and Masaka. North of Kabalega Falls, in Gulu, however, there is a husband and wife medical team from Montreal who still keep a small hospital functioning. Visiting these people is the objective of our journey and, so, instead of going directly to Kampala, we go northward and circle counter clockwise through Masindi and Gulu and Kasese on to the eastern edge of the Ruwenzoris, the "Mountains of the Moon".

Our first visit is with Drs. Lucille Teasdale and Piero Corti at St. Mary's Hospital just outside of Gulu at Lacor. Lucille is a Canadian from Montreal, her husband from Italy; they both refuse to leave their patients and return to safety. We have brought them large boxes of laundry soap, salt, lamp kerosene, flour and sugar as well as a little coffee and milk powder. The small hospital is an oasis of peace and order. There are still a few nurses in training who have not fled back to their villages, or perhaps who have no homes to which to return. Morning clinics are busy but people are afraid to come, a foreign run hospital is a target for military troops, and a destination for military wounded. In the cooking pot for dinner is dried corn and red beans, no onions, no salt, no meat.

The climate of Uganda is as close to perfect as it gets; days of warm sunshine with light showers in the afternoon and cool nights unbroken by harsh seasons of cold or wet. The altitude takes the edge off the tropical heat and rain. It is true that here, if you erect a fence from freshly cut poles, the poles will sprout roots and become trees. Many of the banana, cocoa, sugar and coffee plantations have returned to a jungle state after their owners fled the irrational violence.

Only three things seem to flourish in nature under Idi Amin: vegetation, weaver birds and hippos. The evil that flourishes is not part of this article. Doubtless the Nile perch are enjoying a respite from sport fishermen as well, but the tourist infrastructure has ground to a near halt and none of the lodges can offer the rare visitor either land or water safaris.

This is not to say that the lodges are closed. We are offered accommodation everywhere we stop for the night and, in fact, are always offered a menu and food at country inns when we halt for lunch or a rest. However, the depressing reality is that, although the impeccable service and hospitality of a flourishing tourist industry remain, there is nothing else left.

We arrive, for example, at the Mweya Safari Lodge at the edge of the Ruwenzori Mountains at dinner time. The receptionist, the porters, the parking valets, the maitre d' and the waiters are efficient and polite. The table is set with white linen and sterling silver and the five-course menu is newly hand printed and placed into its embossed leather folder. The menu contains five courses—all variations on fried or mashed bananas, the local staple, called matoki. Some of the dishes may have been made from sweet bananas but mostly these are cooking bananas or plantain.

The waiter offers us fried Nile perch which we knew he must have expected to eat himself for his dinner, although he denies it vigorously. The staff cannot have been paid for years yet they continue to carry out their duties. It may be that Amin's security people stay here.

Despite Uganda's potential for producing food, during this time of Idi Amin many people are close to starving, or at least severely malnourished, because the main source of protein is the ubiquitous matoki which is high in carbohydrates and low in protein. They also grow groundnuts, peanuts to Canadians, which are higher in protein but not high enough to prevent malnutrition.

In Kenya, the common food is ugali, or posho, which is a cornmeal product similar to polenta from Italy and grits from the southern United States. It is made from ground maize and water and varies in consistency from porridge to thick dough. Maize sold in East Africa is not the sweet corn we savour in Canada, it is hard and starchy. Often sold along the roadside, roasted over an open fire pit, it provides a cheap filling snack.

It is difficult to know how to react to all the pomp and circumstance at the lodge as we are the only guests in the two hundred room hotel, sit at the only table laid in an enormous dining room filled with empty tables and an entire hotel staff with nothing to do but wait on us.

After dinner we are lit to our room in a far corner of the building by a porter who runs ahead screwing and unscrewing a single light bulb into the successive empty receptacles. When he leaves us at our doorway, he presents us with the bulb but admonishes us not to waste it by telling us glowing accounts of the sights an early riser might encounter. He also solemnly unwinds and hands us our ration of toilet paper, about six squares each. In the room, the mattresses are more luxurious than those of any Sheraton, but the sheets are much mended and threadbare. It is painfully obvious that when any item is finished or broken, it cannot be replaced or fixed. It is equally obvious that the staff are people of pride and are producing miracles of service and courtesy.

The following morning, we take a boat trip along the Kazinga Channel to view any wild game that come to the banks to drink. Two monitor lizards, several dozen bobbing hippo and thousands of weavers swooping in and out of their swaying nests comprise the morning's head count.

Reportedly, in 1974, herds of large antelope and gazelle still roamed the plains, elephant numbered around 3,000 and large cats were still common. Eighteen months later, we see nothing in any of the parks except one old Cape buffalo. The hippos alone represent the vast herds of large game. Idi's troops have shot them all with their automatic weapons for food or fun, mostly fun.

Even though the effects of civil war are felt in the countryside, the promise of agricultural and natural bounty creates an illusion of peace and abundance. Nearer to Kampala, the disruption and devastation cannot be covered up. Many fields are untended, the Ankole cattle are scrawny and few in number, nobody waves or smiles and it seems wiser not to take any photographs. We make no effort to talk to them, we do not want to be the cause of their torture or death.

At a school in Masaka, an hour's drive southwest of Kampala, we are welcomed but advised not to stay the night. At the hotel in Kampala we are followed up the elevator by secret policemen. The day after we visit Makerere University, fifteen students are arrested and several killed. The French Ambassador's residence is next to a popular internment compound and during dinner one can hear shouting and screaming. On the way back to Kenya, we are stopped at gun point and forced to transport two armed soldiers. Two weeks after our return to Nairobi, two of the priests we had visited were arrested and thrown out of the country where they had worked for more than twenty years.

At no time are we treated roughly or rudely. There are demands for visas and passports, and checks for identification but we are never delayed unduly, perhaps in deference to the diplomatic license plates and passports, or perhaps because Ugandans are by nature and heritage a polite, friendly people. From recent history, this would not seem to be the case but my experience with individual Ugandans has created an impression of intelligent, diligent, creative people with no particular chip on their shoulder.

The generous natural bounty of the country and climate has created a garden nation. Uganda could feed, if not the globe, at least much of starving Africa. Nature is more forgiving than the human race and if given the opportunity much of the damage could be recouped.

For me, this trip personifies the most difficult dilemma of foreign service life abroad; to see what could be and accept what will be.

Beetles

Keekorock, Kenya, 1976

With its iridescent carapace glinting in the African sunshine, the ungainly beetle lumbers unhesitatingly over the edge of the concrete staircase. The fall tumbles it onto its back and stuns it into temporary immobility. Slowly it begins waving its legs, clawing at the air in a random excess of energy that eventually tips it over onto its belly again. Unerringly and unhesitatingly, it resumes its journey to the edge of the next step and plunges over.

There are seventeen more steps leading down to the lawns below and another hundred metres of tough grass before the beetle can regain its natural habitat on the sparse savannah. As a gesture of interspecies generosity, I pick up the beetle and carry it down to the lawn where it promptly turns around and tackles the staircase from the other direction. Some creatures find it impossible to accept a helping hand.

Over the years, other than people, beetles have provided me more entertainment than any other creature I have encountered. In many respects the two species are not dissimilar. Preset. Single minded. Crusty. Lumbering into flight at unpredictable moments.

Beetles are the quintessential straight line thinker. If it is possible to climb over a mountain, they will not go around. If their pathway lies across the auto route, they will not alter their journey. Not for them the unpredictable existence of the devil–may-care creative mind; they belong to the group of dogged doers.

Beetles can fly, but not gracefully; beetles can crawl, but not with the grace of a balletic chameleon; they can even walk on water if the surface tension is strong enough. If bees had not already commandeered the adjective "bumble", beetles would have. Lack of finesse by no means implies lack of effectiveness. Indeed, just the opposite is true. Beetles are most effective at finding and maintaining their special niches in the most adverse of conditions. They live throughout the world, except for Antarctica, and have been doing so for at least 265 million years, however, they are most numerous in the tropics.

Often solitary, they usually pursue their daily routine with neither encouragement nor distraction from their fellow beetles. However, in the right conditions, they sometimes congregate in masses of millions.

My first encounter with beetles en masse occurred during a rainy season safari to Meru Melika Lodge in northern Kenya. It was evening by the time we had arrived and the dense African night hid all but the most prominent features. Our cabin was a darker shadow among the bushes and we trod carefully along the crushed gravel path, ears alert for ominous rustlings and slitherings.

A night bird screeched but the crunch of the stone underfoot drowned out other sounds. The bearer turned on the porch light and I looked over my shoulder to check on the others. As I did so, the gravel stones stood up and started to walk toward me.

Tan and black, shoulder to shoulder, hundreds of thousands of thumbnail-sized beetles were on the march—and the lodge, including my hut, was in their path.

Guided by an invisible internal map, they were undeterred in their progression through the dining room, across the grounds and through the cluster of cabins. We dined by match light as candles inspired them to flight and they would swan dive into the beer or half gainer into the stew. Needless to say, drinks were sieved through one's teeth and food crunchier than custard was put back onto the plate. Once back in the cabin, the problem was no simpler—how to get them out of the bed and me into it.

Smug and snug an hour later, I thought I had succeeded. In the morning, between the mosquito netting and the mattress were exactly the correct number of beetles to make one single line, head to tail, around the bed between the mattress and the mosquito netting with no extras and no spaces. I was an island in a ring of beetles. Getting up took some finesse. Next door, one son sat with his knees hugged to his chest waiting to be rescued, the other one was quietly flicking them one by one onto the floor where he smacked them with his boot.

Solitary beetles can create their own excitement, too. Prior to dinner at Keekorock Lodge, it is the custom for guests to gather in front of the fireplace for a little aperitif. Guests at safari lodges are a varied assortment of beings from hardened voyeurs to eager neophytes but always among the collection are several for whom nature in the buff is a shock.

Rhino beetles are stubby horned beetles, fascinating for their appearance which is indeed like a horned rhinoceros, but they are lousy fliers even for beetles because of their large size and heavy weight. However, they are the world's strongest creatures for their size and are difficult to shake off when they grab on to ones shirts or trousers. They are commonly several centimetres in length, shiny shelled and fearless. Like all nocturnal insects they are drawn to lights. I have chosen a seat from which I can watch the edges of the lawns through the window as game often come close at night. However, it is not lions that capture my interest; instead, I watch a straying rhino beetle climb cumbrously up the curtains, across the arm of the sofa and up the sweater of a lady with hair combed out like a lion's mane, blond hair that catches the light.

When it reaches her hair, the climbing becomes more difficult and little tugs are necessary before it can proceed. The blond merely moves her head a little, then she twitches her shoulders and tugs her sweater tighter thinking it is the breeze through the open window. Gradually it becomes obvious to her that breezes do not tweak one's hair like a lover, anyway, her current one is standing beside the fireplace several metres away. She reaches up to smooth away the distracting sensation.

The smoothing hand encounters the beetle which instinctively wraps its legs around her finger and tightens its grip. She turns her head. Her eyes widen, her mouth opens and she emits a scream that could have been bottled. Close up a rhino beetle is awesome and ugly.

She leaps to her feet, her gin and tonic flying in one direction and her hair in the other. The wondrous mane is a glamorous wig covering her safari crew cut. The beetle takes off, straight into the face of an amused guest for whom the humour of the situation rapidly dissipates. In the general confusion, the beetle escapes into the night, probably to write beetle books on the irrational reactions of human beings. I am no help. My assurances that the rhino beetle is a perfectly harmless vegetarian fall on deaf ears.

We end up eating dinner in a stifling dining room with the windows firmly shut. However, there are many smiling waiters.

This is not to imply that I was born with beetle cool. On the contrary, at one of our first diplomatic dinners, beetles played a prominent role. We had been welcomed with warmth and cold juices in the elegant drawing room of a wealthy Indian. During this hour of conviviality, beetles with sticky coats barged into lamps and guests, apparently unremarked by everyone except me. Dinner was served in near darkness out on the lawn. It was impossible to see what was on the plate and eating was done mostly by feel.

Seated in honour beside my hostess, I munched along determinedly. However, I had not forgotten the beetles and when I bit down on a walnut-sized piece with an exterior shell it was too much. There was no way I was going to swallow it, yet I did not feel that expelling it precipitously onto the lawn would be in good taste. My first lesson in diplomatic cool. I coughed it into the serviette, dropped the bundle accidentally on the grass and drank deeply of my G&T, the blazes with amoebas lurking in the ice.

Sometime later I came across the spice, black cardamom, and realized that it must have been that and not a beetle that I had spit into the linen napkin. To this day, I do not like crunchy surprises in my food.

A Paean to Pleasures Past

Robinson's Island, Kenya, 1977

Many times in life one meets memorable people. People who hear and walk to their own drummer, who persistently go their own way and live according to their own philosophy. Such a person is David Hurd. He is not a person we know well but someone whose dream will provide one of our lasting memories.

I had heard of him from colleagues at the Kenya National Museum where I volunteered. He is one of the hundreds of white Kenyans who consider Kenya their home and live suspended between the old colonial world and modern Kenya. David has the distinction of being the only person to be kidnapped by Somali poachers and released alive. He is passionate about the environment and despairs at the destruction affecting the forests, rivers and reefs of his country.

In an effort to prove one can live within the bounty of, and in harmony with, the environment, he has built a unique restaurant on an isolated stretch of Kenyan coast north of Mombasa. One of our most memorable meals is eaten there.

Kiny'Ole is a slinky sand dune separated from the mangrove swamp by an opportunistic sea channel. To rename it Robinson's Island requires considerable idealistic optimism and a penchant to emulate the life of Robinson Crusoe. To establish a four star restaurant miles from the nearest village, over rutted dirt road in the back of beyond of a little third world nation on this same shifting sand pile, takes colossal chutzpah. Not only do patrons have to arrive by Landrover, or light plane, or boat, they have to hot foot it over burning sand and sit on wooden stools at rough slab tables under a flapping thatch roof.

Inconspicuous to the point of invisibility, one could have passed within one hundred feet of the entire establishment—restaurant, gardens, parking lot, kitchens, landing strip and all—without seeing it. No road signs point the way. No map carries the location. Slumping casually into shifting sand, the wood and thatch structure could easily be the abandoned retreat of Defoe's hero.

To get the maitre de's attention, one parks on the opposite bank, clangs an old ship's bell and waits for the punt to be poled across. But once there, sheltered from the unceasing wind and scouring sand by a wall of woven palm fronds, guests can gorge and feast and stuff until they can scarcely stagger to the string cots provided for their recovery.

Its founder, owner, manager, architect and chief cook is an eccentric remnant of the colonial period named David Hurd. Taking time out of a chequered career as a latter-day Dennis Finch-Hatton, he has engineered Robinson's Island as a unique experiment in total harmony between enterprise and environment. David is host, chef and maître de, only and ably assisted by a local fisherman who catches the menu of the day.

Tables, stools, cots, roof and walls, all are hand-crafted from local trees and vines; plates and bowls are from local wood, cups are designed of coconut shell, decorations are of coral and shell and free for the making. Not only the building but the food it serves comes from the immediate environment. Everything on the menu either grows on the island or lives in the waters around it except the necessary alcoholic beverages. No electricity. No plumbing. Nothing imported or purchased except a small selection of whisky, rum, gin and fresh water for guests and a gas fridge to keep the ice intact.

The array and abundance of menu choices depends entirely on the results of the fisherman's morning catch and the state of David's melon patch. On the morning tide the fisherman paddles out to the reef in his dugout, snorkel mask and fishing spear in hand, to harvest the offerings of the nearby coral formations of the fringing reef that bejewels the Kenyan coast. Augmented with the versatile coconut, these sources never fail to provide a five-course meal of exquisite delicacy and infinite variety.

For nibbles with a pre-dinner Glenlivet or Heineken, there are deep-fried coconut or banana chips or groundnuts roasted in their shells; for appetizers one may feast on raw or grilled rock oysters with grated coconut followed by steamed lobster or crab. Mullet, rubbed with spice and grilled over an open fire, might make the main course. If one is still hungry a yam curry guarantees to fill the empty spaces. For dessert there is vine-ripened melon with lime and hot, strong Arabica coffee sweetened with coconut milk. A dark roasted coffee bean held lightly between the teeth during sips of cognac added an exotic pungency to an indulgent end to an indulgent meal.

Such delicious safari coffee is made over an open fire, usually in a conical blue enameled coffee pot balanced carefully on several stones in a bed of ashes. Think of the coffee pots in old western movies. Into the pot one puts a tablespoon of freshly ground coffee beans for each cup of coffee plus one for the pot, adds cold water, a cup for each spoonful of ground coffee. When it comes to a boil and starts to bubble, it is removed from the heat and allowed to settle. Repeat twice more. After it settles the final time, it is served with hot condensed milk or, in the case of Robinson's Island, thick coconut milk. The rich sweet milk is hot, left to heat on the side of the fire pit while the coffee makes. If you try this, remember to punch holes in the tin of condensed milk first, otherwise it may take off in a spray of sticky Eagle Brand glory.

We drive in from Vipingo, a village two hours south of Kiny'Ole where we are vacationing in a rented beach house; the other guests that day fly in from Mombasa in a small plane and land on the beach. The timing of the meal is determined by the tide as the plane can only land and take off at low tide. It is a crew of an Air France flight who are on their way up the coast to overnight in Lamu between flights. A dhow moves serenely past on the turquoise Indian Ocean, a dugout canoe rests on its side next to the plane on the hard sand beach, a leaky punt on the landside canal separates us from our Land Rover shimmering in the hot shade of a kapok tree while a local monkey troop uses it for a siesta and we do not even blink an eye, this is Africa. We are resting quietly on rope cots, recovering from our indulgence and dozing away the heat of the afternoon sun.

Impeccably fresh seafood, slow-simmered curry, sun-hot melon served in a setting of wild beauty on an uninhabited tropical beach—no black tie extravaganza nor haute cuisine restaurant will ever surpass the sensual pleasures of dinner at Robinson's Island.

Elephants on Parade

Nairobi, March, 1978

All things considered, I feel that four flat tires on my car is an acceptable outcome to this afternoon's adventure. It could have been otherwise.

We are on safari in Samburu National Game Park in northern Kenya. Safaris are quite routine in East Africa. By 1978 I am an old hand at this. I know my flora and fauna, I carry maps and emergency gear and feel savvy at the ways of walking on the wild side, at least in the bush near the lodge. I expected no trouble; however, I should have known that such a moment is exactly when trouble pays a visit.

After the hundredth ostrich and the thousandth zebra, even the short term visitors to Kenya opt for the swimming pool and a cold beer. In this case, the men and the boys opted for the beer and pool back at Samburu Lodge while we women and girls set out along the sandy trails once again.

The women in this case were I, a friend visiting from Hong Kong and her two young daughters. Rejecting the hard-to-drive Land Rover with the front door that swings open on curves, we pile into my little yellow Volkswagen Polo and set out to capture some game with our cameras. The map was quite clear about our route and had proved reliable yesterday. We wave gaily and promise to be back before sundown.

The rains have been abundant this year. The elephant grass is taller than the elephants; the baobabs and the desert rose are in fleeting flower; the wildlife is well fed, content and unafraid.

Bored with the main track, we switch to a side trail. The well worn ruts straddle a grassy strip which is easily drivable and, in a short distance, it will rejoin the main track.

The track weaves around a grassy knoll and abruptly converges with several other trails which lead out over the dry, crusty bed of a seasonal gully. In a rainstorm, this gully will fill with water in mere minutes, washing away anything in its path but today it looks benign. I inch the front tires onto the sand and then, in a rush of caution, I decide to take a test foray on foot to see how solid it really is. It is open land, high noon, everything hungry should be sleeping.

Within two steps I am breaking through the dry crust and sinking to my ankles. The dry looking river bed is full of sugar sand, unstable and undrivable. I soft foot it back to the car and back up gently onto the harder track as smoothly as I can. Fortunately, there is only an inch or two of the sand on top of the harder under pan.

We choose one of the other trails and complete a short circuit that leads us back to the same spot where we intend to follow our previous route back to the lodge. The animal watching has been good and I am pleased with myself. Dik-dik, oryx, Grevy's zebra and reticulated giraffe are all safely captured on film. The huge baobab trees are in bloom and the bird life is active with breeding antics in full swing. As we sit in a lay-by near the sugar sand trail consulting our map, a low-slung red sports car driven by two fashionably outfitted men roars past. With a flourish, they back up, ask directions about the road ahead and, totally ignoring our warning about the river bed, whip off in a shower of dust along the trail that ends in the sugar sand river crossing.

"Maybe we should check, just to make sure they got across okay?"

We look at each other. It is starting to get late but in this part of the park it is unlikely other cars will be passing. Smug with my naive knowledge of jungle craft, and unmindfully ignoring the predatory potential in the surrounding grass and overhanging trees in the coming dusk, we retrace our route to the previous crossing. Sure enough. There they are, three metres from the edge, up to their hubs in sand and digging deeper.

"Need any help?" I call out the window.

"Nein, nein", comes the answer.

We watch until their axle sinks into the sugar like stuff. What I should have done was head back to the Lodge and report the situation. What I do is take the floor mats out of my car, whip them efficiently into place in front of their rear wheels and say, "Try it now".

With a throaty, low gear growl and acceleration that flings the mats a metre into the air, they depart without a backward glance or an arm up flung in gratitude. I don't stay to see if they make the other side safely.

"I wonder where they're going?"

"Sure in a hurry."

"I'm sure they appreciated our help, though."

Well, all this has made us late and, having no desire to be caught by the implacable African nightfall, I waste no time locating the nearest main track. In high spirits and full of satisfaction at having had a splendid afternoon, I pull smartly out of the side trail, accelerate onto the main track. And stand on the brakes. No time even to shout. Maps, water canteens, binoculars and passengers slide onto the floor.

We have crashed, uninvited, into a late afternoon gathering of the local elephant clans. They have been standing quietly along the edges of the trail, hidden by the ridge and luxuriant elephant grass. The corn in Oklahoma has nothing on this stuff; this stuff really does hide elephants. Retreat is in order. Impossible. A large matriarch has stepped into the road behind us and stands staring into the rear window. I now realize how small a VW really is; I am staring at her knee caps.

Forward. I smash the gears through their paces. Not fast enough. Faster than a speeding bullet would not have been fast enough. In front of us, a yearling calf has slid down the little embankment and into the road ahead of us. Frightened by his precipitate separation from his mother, he is squealing and thrashing about, trying to climb back to her side. If our unexpected arrival hadn't upset them, this has. Mother and aunts are agitated and flapping their huge ears at us. Swaying and trumpeting, they express their desire for us to be gone. Believe me, our wishes coincide. Grass as high as an elephant's eye is higher still in a little Volkswagen.

Just as things are getting really tense, the little fellow has a momentary success and I shoot out of there without discussing it first. The whole episode takes maybe ten seconds. Even the girls forget to scream. Thank goodness, that would really have upset the elephants.

Anyway, that's how I get the flat tires. The nearest exit is under a group of thorn trees. These trees are not misnamed. These are the same three inch thorns some tribes use to close gaping wounds and pierce leather. I can personally tell you that they also pierce tires.

The return is somewhat circuitous, the direct route being back through the elephants and the map being somewhat misleading. On this leg of the trip we do not stop for sightseeing, by now the African night is descending and no one knows where we are. Relief is shared by us all when we arrive back at the lodge. No one notices the damage to the tires until the next morning. Even when I explain, my husband does not understand how I could drive twenty kilometres on four flat tires and not notice.

It wasn't that I hadn't noticed; I simply had no intention of stopping.

WASHINGTON, DC : 1978-1982

After three years in East Africa, we are cross posted to the United States. By seeking a cross posting at this stage we could reasonably hope to be back in Ottawa by the time our boys reached the end of junior high school. To go home at this point probably would have meant leaving them behind at a residential school in their late teens which we did not want to do. So, Washington was the compromise transition.

It allowed us to reunite with family in Canada and introduce our sons to their Canadian relations. It provided a similar educational system, an introduction into North American culture—especially adolescent culture—and an chance for them to understand what being a Canadian entailed, a chance for them to live and ordinary life and not that of a privileged dip brat (not that mine were brats, of course).

We reveled in North Atlantic beaches, camping in the mountains, cross-country skiing and learning to ice skate, crab and corn boils, Thanksgiving and Easter celebrations and the freedom from being constantly on parade. We could be ordinary people, something which one has to work at when exposed to the artificially entitled life of a foreign diplomatic posting. I have sadly observed some of my colleagues' failure to grasp that the privilege belongs to the position, not to the person.

An Illusory Similarity

Washington, DC, November, 1978

A posting to Washington, DC, is either sought or avoided. A taste for exotic places does not interest some diplomats and it does offer solutions to some foreign service issues: education for children and parents, career training opportunities, nearness to elderly parents left behind in Canada, decent weather and good roads, familiarity and proximity to home. Others seek it out as a career move. Washington, DC, is, after all, the centre of world political decision making and commerce. For those intrigued by the machinations of politicians, presidents, journalists, lobbyists and media moguls and mavens, it is the place to be.

Washington has something for everyone but, because of the large size of the mission, the feeling of community is missing. Canadians at the embassy can travel back and forth to Canada for the holidays and their vacations, talk freely and make friends with their new neighbours, shop at will and suffer from a plethora of consumer goods instead of a deficit. Daily life is very similar to that in Ottawa. It is easier to maintain ties with Canadian life and friends; hence, less effort is put into creating a Canadian community within the mission.

Policy wonks at headquarters in Ottawa reckon that embassy staff do not need assistance when they rotate into the USA and, therefore, offers none. We find our own accommodation—pending HQ approval of course—and ship down our own furniture, remove our cars from storage, put our children into local schools and are governed by American regulations as everyone else. The only diplomatic privilege is our tax exempt card given to all diplomatic personnel. The anonymity is actually a relief after the lack of it in Kenya.

At first, it seems much like Ottawa only larger, faster, more diverse. Ottawa times ten. The differences sneak up on one and can come as a shock. One feels a half beat off the measure and it is hard to define the reason.

Is their oft expressed patriotism a little too exhibitionistic? Do they make private tragedy public? Do they grieve too publicly? Do they fawn over public people too mindlessly? Do they create unworthy celebrities too readily? Are they too proud of their prejudices? Do they lack the hubris of a truly civilized people? Is their world view obnoxiously

Amerocentric? Are their media too crass? Do I view Canada through rose coloured glasses? Is it just culture shock again?

It is a difficult place in which to maintain the Canadian point of view, habits and values. It is overwhelmingly American, especially in school classes like history, literature, civics and early education. My boys are being penalized for not knowing Sesame Street and Disney movies. Approaching junior high school and not familiar with TV? Tut, tut. Well, sorry, there wasn't a lot of TV in Africa and we have gone to a great deal of effort to encourage the best of Canadian traditions in our children.

As usual, the things I do not know are embarrassingly many. The most blatant is that the population of the District of Columbia is predominantly black and that this fact is never forgotten by anyone. After three years in India and three years in Africa, for the first time racial prejudice becomes a problem. Not that prejudice did not exist there but now it is a daily presence in our lives. After attending school with students from forty nations and playing with children whose skin colour ranged from the paleness of Finland to the ebony of Sudan, choosing pals based on colour is a shock to our children. That blacks would do the same to them is equally confusing and distressing.

In the end, except for the overt racial prejudice, it isn't that different from Ottawa. Not that Ottawa does not have prejudice; however, it is more covert, less obvious to those not on the receiving end.

Ottawa has 24 Sussex and the Hill; Washington has 1600 Pennsylvania and the Hill.

Historically, both are built on locations arbitrarily selected for military and political reasons to avoid choosing between already established sites and both are built on swamps.

Geographically, both depend on bridges to keep their functioning halves together; both are conscious of the "across the river" syndrome.

Culturally, both are considered by other, flashier cities to be slightly behind the times and conservative; both consider themselves to be intellectual and cultural centres.

Ethnically, both have been less influenced by waves of immigration than other large urban centres and, therefore, are bastions of "founding fathers thinking". [This is no longer true of Ottawa which has benefited from several recent influxes of refugees from the Middle East and Africa.]

Bureaucratically, both are civil service dominated and politician inundated.

Architecturally, Washington is a collection of Greek and Roman wedding cakes, the offspring of a late nineteenth century lust for Athens and Rome. Porticoes and Ionic columns, saucer domes and inset-arches, improbable balconies and wrought iron curlicues amaze and amuse thousands of visitors each year. Ottawa is more Victorian except for its Parliament buildings. Both are dotted with large contemporary hulks.

Conceived and built originally as a place where Congress would meet during the cool months, Washington emerged from the mud of the Potomac and Anacostia rivers on the backs of black labour as a neutral zone independent of state influence. Ottawa was conceived as a military safe house and became a den of lumber barons on the backs of Irish and immigrant labour.

Despite malaria and yellow fever which are now eradicated, dank, dreary winters and infernally hot summers which are not, the cities survived and gradually acquired the accoutrements of modern political prestige: beautiful libraries, universities, medical research centres, cultural centres and theatres, armies of lawyers and lobbyists and a massive bureaucracy. In spring people come to Ottawa for the tulips and to Washington for the cherry trees, in between the tourists come to gawk or protest.

Washington, DC, is a city whose budget is controlled by Congress and administered by an elected mayor and city council, and whose residents could not vote in presidential elections until 1964. The past has been carefully preserved in museums, collections, heritage homes, statuary and painting. Ottawa is young enough it has just begun to preserve its history.

Washington, District of Columbia, repository of the hopes and dreams, aspirations and dilemmas of 236 million Americans and their neighbours, allies and partners. People, politicians and power, that is the game in Washington and, like any sport, the game has its players, spectators, commentators and groupies. Not the least among these are the members of what is probably the world's largest diplomatic corps.

What is their game?

Like the augurs of old, these declared diplomats, and their interspersed spies, seek the omens among the vapours wafting from the American political and policy cauldron that might affect their own countries. Contacts and access within the bubbling cauldron is the daily routine; interpretation of vague omens, intentions and the deceptions of political discourse make the game intensely problematic.

Who among the 535 members of Congress is worth the candle? Who is up and who is out in the Administration? Is the State Department more important than Defense on a particular issue? These fleetingly heavy issues furrow the brows of diplomats, friend or foe alike. And if the morass of drifting currents and sinkholes leaves one stranded, the high priced, temporarily out-of-office gunslingers on K Street—lobbyists—can be bought to bring enlightenment and credibility to a hungry diplomat.

At the end of four years we go home.

OTTAWA : 1982-1989

Back home to live after seven years. The boys were now young teenagers. After seven years away from the Canadian winter they needed jackets and boots, skates and skis, adult beds and desks, separate bedrooms, etc., etc. How to manage all these expenses? Relocation allowances cover a tiny portion. Haven't you been saving for this? Yeah, sure. They weren't the only things needing the love that money can buy, the house needed a roof, seven years of tenants had also left the house in need of paint and floor refurbishing—a hundred here, a thousand there.

That was the money side of coming home.

The other side was the mental adjustment, more difficult and potentially more personally costly. This period of adjustment is called re-entry and is the flip side of exiting. Together they comprise the two adaptation cycles of foreign service rotationality, leaving home and returning home.

My constant worry was how to help the boys feel at home in a home they barely remembered. They were five and seven years old when we left Ottawa, twelve and fourteen now. Another set of friends to leave behind and another set of friends to make; another unwritten set of school and social codes to decipher.

I had been trying over the years to maintain their Canadian roots and loyalties and traditions: Christmas routines, Halloween parties,

Valentine's Day, family birthdays, family connections and memories. This would be the test. At least I could help them look like everyone else, hence, the clothing bills.

As for us parents, being back at headquarters provided its own re-entry shock. We weren't used to such close departmental supervision; the post abroad at least gave one the illusion of independence. We had also forgotten the less than global mindset of ordinary Ottawans prevalent among our neighbours and non-rotational colleagues. We wanted to fit in, too; we needed to regain a feeling of comfort in our Canadian skins. Seven years away had skewed our memories.

The Petard of Equity

As a woman, one of the social tides I had watched from a foreign eddy was the surging and retreating waves of the feminist movement. The pressure to work for money, as versus volunteer or work as a homemaker, was omnipresent and persistent. The value of being a stay-at-home mother, working full time raising the children versus being a "working woman" outside the home—volunteering does not count—was in full spate in these years.

It has not quite faded even yet. What has changed is the acceptance that it is a legitimate choice to be either. Employers are cooperating to a greater extent, both partners share in the decision and ensuing responsibilities and there are more childcare options for most families. If the article sounds full of angst, remember that all that angst led to today's opportunities. It's not a perfect world but it is much more equitable than it was twenty-five years ago. And the responsibilities keep growing.

Ottawa, January, 1984

When a women asks the question, "And what do you do?" to another woman, the meaning depends on the situation.

When asked to a man, it is meant literally. The questioner wants to know whether the person is a banker, a realtor or a journalist. When asked to another woman the meaning is quite different.

What the question really means is, "Do you have a paying job outside the home and, if so, how does it stack up against mine?" Homemakers never ask the question.

What the questioner is assessing is her success as measured in remuneration and job profile. She wants to know how she measures up. Top marks would go to a bilingual single mother in a high paying non-traditional job who manages male workers and has the figure and face of Cher. This answer would lead to an in-depth comparison of hours of overtime, travel tips and an exchange of business cards before they each run off to relieve the child caregiver who must be home by eleven.

Bottom marks would go to a unilingual married mother who stays at home to care for school age children. The implications and assumptions in this answer are many and damning. To be unilingual, especially anglophone, is to be politically incorrect as well as unsophisticated, rural and culturally boorish. Married might be acceptable if it is a second marriage and there is an implication of a career merely suspended, otherwise there is a suspicion of hopeless dependence and lack of spine. Staying at home implies lack of ambition, lack of ability and lack of character unless one can hint at personal wealth, failing health or a book being written. To be dedicated to the care of school age children (as versus pre-school infants) sends out signals of smother-mothering and whining brats whose independent learning curve is being stunted.

The answer to this question will determine the course of the ensuing conversation. If a woman works for money outside the home, it is assumed that she can discuss current affairs, politics, the economy, the cultural life of Ottawa versus Paris, and generally participate in intellectual intercourse.

If the answer is no, then conversation reverts to the weather and the assumption that the only type of intercourse of which she is capable is sexual. As an observation though, I will say, it is difficult to avoid women's conversation turning to baby bearing and child rearing, perhaps it is the one sure thing we have in common. I have childless friends who say this is a conversational cross they must often endure.

Not only is this demeaning, it is unjust. Unjust to assume that a woman who is not in the labour force is incapable of intellectual pursuits and unjust to the skills required to make a home.

A home is not a house which serves as a motel for transient family members. A home is where people share their lives and gather strength from the sharing; a place of respite and nurture which acts as a fortress against the buffets and strains of the outside world; a place where children learn to savour the smell of baking bread and stir the Christmas pudding; a place where they learn to share, to trust, to feel good about themselves and accept responsibility for their actions; a place where the generations can meet and grow to respect each other.

It is a fallacy to assume that anyone can make a home.

Homemaking requires the same skills that it takes to run a successful business or manage an effective government department. Put into terms used in the workplace, it takes personnel administration and management, financial management and accounting, specific knowledge, training skills, supervisory skills, public relations and interpersonal communications skills and hours of unpaid overtime. These are only for starters, the basics upon which the homemaker builds. There are no courses that teach generosity of spirit, compassion and respect for difference, strength of conviction and commitment to the future.

Homemaking and motherhood are two of the most tasking jobs in the world, yet most women accept the challenge unprepared and ignorant of the demands. When they do succeed through experience and sacrifice, they are unrewarded and unrecognized.

The stakes are high. The future of the species depends on their success. The young of the human race take over twenty years to reach maturity and no one has devised a better method of ensuring their maturation than the tutelage of parents in the home. With no example to follow, how will they know what to do when their turn comes?

In the effort to release women from the bonds of domestic servitude and male domination, there is a danger of throwing the baby out with the bath water, of forcing women from one untenable position to another. From one in which they cannot leave the home to one in which they cannot stay in it.

Women bear the children. Science has not yet circumvented that process although it has tampered with it. Until men give birth they will not accept an equal role in child rearing; they will help, but they will not accept ultimate responsibility. When the chips are down, it will be the women who guard the future of the race.

The pressure for women to be financially and emotionally independent of other people makes the choice of dedicated child rearing a courageous one. There is precious little support for either decision. If a woman stays at home she risks poverty in the event of marital breakdown and the family risks total financial dependence on a single income. She may find herself the only mother on the block and regarded as a parasite on the national purse. If she pursues a career, who will raise the children and build the home? Her partner becomes threatened and departs in search of self and love, i.e., love for himself, her children take up residence in the mall and her boss thinks there are twenty-four hours in a day, a situation similar to building a budget based on gross rather than net income.

The fact that the question, "What do you do?" has so many interpretations is revealing. It is referred to as that awful question, or that dreaded question, because of the anxiety stirred up in formulating the answer. Women find themselves justifying accepting part time work, or working sporadically from home, or creating fictitious plans for starting a business or returning to work, or apologizing for taking time off to raise children or fulfill family obligations.

Freedom to choose is the issue here, and the right to have that choice respected and supported within the family and in the larger societal context. In the struggle for individual rights and gender equity in the workplace, the family is the loser.

By the way, to be "hoisted on one's own petard" means to be hurt by a plan or device one intended for self benefit. The women's movement is our petard.

Win, Lose or Draw

As do many professions, the foreign service suffers from poor media relations. Diplomacy is of necessity carried out behind closed doors, with discretion bordering on secrecy. Generally, diplomatic successes are credited to politicians while the failures are laid squarely on the shoulders of the diplomats, deserved or not. The role of diplomats is little understood. Consequently, they are often ridiculed, vilified and misrepresented in the press. They are easy targets. They are not allowed to defend themselves and are often forbidden to talk to the media.

The relationship between the department and the government is frequently strained, fraught with lack of trust and misunderstanding, jealousy even. Certainly the two groups routinely feel that the other one is ignorant of the true situation and cannot be trusted to act appropriately. In the brief periods when both sides are cooperating, Canada benefits in big and small ways. Treaties, agreements and accords that allow the movement of people, the international flow of goods and services and multilateral cooperation flourish. Such agreements allow Canadians to travel without hassle; they allow lumber, wheat, textiles and food products to be sold and bought on the global market; they allow foreign adoptions to proceed; they allow foreign aid to reach the destitute and the internet, for better or worse, to be the great information equalizer.

This was written twenty years ago; if I wrote it today, in 2009, I am not sure much would have changed. Certainly, the relationship between the elected government and the professional foreign service has not improved and lack of respect on both sides seriously hinders the work of Canadian diplomats.

Ottawa, February, 1985

"Here we go again," I think, as dark tentacles of persecution wiggle their tips around in my mind. "Just once I wish they'd stick up for us." They being primarily the politicians and the media. Both are groups who should, of all non-foreign service people, understand something of life in the foreign service. The first employ us and the second cover the international news, neither can do their work without entering the arena in which the foreign service works. Naturally enough, if they do not understand the foreign services's professional role, how can they understand the internal policies and regulations that govern our private life?

This self-indulgent outburst is occasioned by a brouhaha over membership in the Aberdeen Boat Club by diplomats at the Canadian High Commission in Hong Kong. As I understand it, access to the club is a result of debentures in the club, a financially sound arrangement worked out which gave, without regard to rank, membership in the club to Canadian personnel at the Hong Kong mission. Not unexpectedly, this tempest in a teapot has been created by journalistic innuendo followed by departmental overreaction.

When the facts are reviewed, it becomes clear that Hong Kong is not Ottawa and different circumstances exist. The superficials of the situation have been judged without all the information, and by Ottawa standards. Quelle surprise!! It doesn't help that the non-rotational personnel of the department are often jealous of the perceived luxury benefits that are available to rotational staff while overseas. This envy is manifest in the no exceptions policy of "no one shall either be advantaged or disadvantaged by a foreign posting" yet policy makers always seem to think we are being advantaged. No wonder we begin to develop a ghetto mentality with its feelings of being misunderstood and persecuted.

Sometimes I think foreign service life should not be undertaken by anyone who cannot live with the "damned if you do, damned if you don't" dilemma. If we live like diplomats, we are wasting public money. If we live like private citizens, we are failing in our diplomatic duty. If we sympathize with the host country, we have lost our perspective. If we promote Canada's interests too avidly, we are insensitive. If we go public, we are compromising security. If we keep silent, we are withholding information. If we advise elected officials, we are interfering. If we keep our own counsel, we are being uncooperative. If we advise action, we are overreacting. If we advise caution, we are old women. If we miss a trick, we are ignorant. Above all, if we should be suspected of having acquired some of the privileges of the "upper classes", we are reprimanded, held up to public criticism and cut off at the knees without so much as an opportunity to make our case. Even those who should know better are guilty of over reacting to the biased insinuations of the public press.

Who are the most demanding of luxury attention abroad? The politicians and the fourth estate. Not only do they demand access to top people and insiders, they expect the attention and treatment of international stars.

Last year's dramatic increase in the shelter share is another case of a Canadian-Ottawa yardstick being applied to the overseas life of the foreign service. Statistics based on two income families do not apply to the majority of our families. In fact, they apply only to employee-couples as no other couple can count on the accompanying spouse being employed even at local salary scales.

Perhaps it is inevitable that the lives and work of rotational personnel are regulated to a large extent by the whims of a non-rotational management and an elected super-structure. But when departmental decisions and actions, taken after full consultation with Treasury Board, can be so readily questioned and overturned, it is an insult to our intelligence and integrity. Another instance of trust versus mistrust that bedevils the relationship between rotational and non-rotational personnel.

This situation probably accounts for more morale problems than any other single factor. It is immaterial whether any given decision is good or bad. It is the feeling of being haphazardly managed by those who have little empathy for, or understanding of, the realities of foreign service life that creates frustration. Many do not seem to understand the purpose and uses of a professional diplomatic corps let alone foreign service life.

[No apologies for the "royal we". Anything that affects family life in the foreign service includes me.]

The eleventh commandment of foreign service management seems to be, "They shall be treated as just another part of the civil service; neither receiving undue benefit, nor suffering any undue losses." Fine— except that many people fail to consider that most foreign service people neither live nor work in Canada. For example, when it is discovered that it costs more to live our normal Canadian lifestyle overseas—to which they say we are entitled—mental consternation and financial constipation set in. One that galls me is that we pay a rent share larger than the costs of running our mortgage free home in Ottawa, utilities included.

The superficial glamour, the temporarily inflated status and the exotic flavour of an overseas posting are thought to be adequate compensation for the disruption in our lives. The image is persuasive and becomes the reality. In all fairness, we do little to disabuse the press and the politicians of this attitude. We hug our specialness to ourselves and perpetuate the myths of our existence. We feel misunderstood and, therefore, make no effort to clarify our work and lifestyle.

We show visitors the best of what our life can offer. We tell inspection teams only the easily quantifiable complaints. We answer reporters in smooth, non-controversial terms on obvious issues. To do otherwise would be perceived by the public, rightly or wrongly, as unjustified complaining.

The truth of the matter is, however, that we spend half our lives adjusting, living and working in unfamiliar surroundings, in unfamiliar cultures, with unfamiliar people in an unfamiliar language. The isolation and hardship is camouflaged by the exotic environment. The loneliness is masked by the official life.

Under bizarre, outrageous conditions we defend, promote and interpret Ottawa's positions and decisions to people who find us equally bizarre and outrageous.

We should not have to apologize for, or continually defend, our need for assistance, often financial, in establishing conditions of service that allow us to maintain a semblance of normality in our lives. There is a difference between a rotational career covering 35 years of one's life, and one or two assignments which cover separate periods of several years. One is a whole lifestyle; the other is an exciting adventure.

Yet to do the work, and to bring our children to competent adulthood, we must remain essentially Canadian in viewpoint and behaviour. We have to adapt to other cultural environments without becoming less a Canadian. For the good of our families, careers and country we cannot afford the more bizarre manifestations of prolonged and repeated relocation shock.

Assisted leave, family reunions, reciprocal working agreements, club memberships and tuition assistance are not perquisites; they are needed cushions against the physical and emotional buffeting that is intrinsic in rotational careers. That being said, there is a fine line between maintaining lifestyle and lining ones pockets—that is where judgment and good sense must prevail. And in the vast majority of cases, it does.

Rites and Rituals

Ottawa, November, 1987

Last Saturday was a normal, breezy Canadian fall day. The kind of day that demands decisions regarding jackets and gloves—to wear or not to wear; to wear now and carry later. Do I need a scarf? Shoes not sandals? And the acceptance that summer clothes must be tidied away for another year.

On that day, the threads of three special celebrations crossed and, in doing so, treated me to one of life's brief moments of confirmation that I might have been doing something right vis-à-vis parenting, something I had been blindly groping through for fourteen years.

My sons and I were enjoying the sights of the Byward Market in the centre of Ottawa and doing some lazy shopping. My older boy was visiting from Queen's University and his brother and I were enjoying his company. These days we didn't often have relaxed time together, time without trains to catch or friends to meet or studies to do. Three minor, everyday events occurred in sequence.

First, the October sun falling on the pumpkins made them glow in a come hither colour.

"Let's make jack-o-lanterns", suggested one. "For Hallowe'en".

"Yeah, let's get two", agreed the other. "So we can each make one, like usual."

Agreement? Between these two? Shared activity?

"Sure," I agreed. "A splendid idea."

Quietly I recalled years when I had had to make this suggestion most strongly in an attempt to instill the Canadian tradition of the jack-o-lantern and then listen while they fussed over who had the biggest, roundest pumpkin

Secondly, we stopped at several market stalls to be sure of having the essential ingredients on hand for Thanksgiving dinner, a Canadian Thanksgiving dinner. I didn't need a list because the menu has not varied in nearly two decades. I've been known to ship tins of cranberry sauce, bags of wild rice and jars of summer savoury half way around the world. Once I even spent a week's grocery money to give a turkey a four-continent tour before it graced our Thanksgiving table in far away India. It had been flown from Canada to Britain to Africa to India. It was a colossal disappointment but that is another story.

I was thinking that maybe I could make a little change in the menu. As I ruminated out loud about maybe having ham instead of turkey, corn pudding instead of stuffing, they each started to add their own must-haves: cranberry sauce, honey glazed carrots, cole slaw without raisins, gravy, mashed potatoes with no lumps…not like every day smashed potatoes.

My younger son added the final mail in the ham coffin.

"You can't stuff a ham," he stated, "and you have to have stuffing for Thanksgiving."

"With savoury," he added.

I must have said that to him once when he was objecting to eating stuffing.

"You can bake ham *and* turkey," one suggested.

"Turkey it is," I announced.

Thirdly, as we nipped into the Bay for a birthday present for my sister, I was disconcerted to walk into an absurdly early Christmas display—decorated trees, twinkling lights, baskets of ornaments, gift wrap and ribbon. When I stopped to consider one of the plastic trees, both boys pulled me away.

"Don't buy one of those. A Christmas tree should be real. I'd rather have no tree than one of those," they told me. "Any kind of tree, just not a plastic one."

With those words I realized that one of my child-rearing goals had been reached. Turkey for Thanksgiving, jack-o-lanterns for Hallowe'en and a real tree for Christmas. How traditionally Canadian can one get? Most of their childhood and early teen years had been spend abroad, far away from familiar Canadian holidays and activities.

Early in our first posting someone had sent me a Canadian magazine which included an article by Pierre Berton. In this article he extolled the value of rites and rituals in building and strengthening a family's sense of itself. He had maintained that, even when separated physically from the family home, by carrying out these traditions one could experience the warmth and feeling of belonging that occurs on close family occasions.

I must have been feeling that New Delhi was very far from home. Usually, Mr. Berton and I do not reach a state of sympatico very quickly but this time his words struck a receptive chord.

There was not much chance of us ever living very close to relatives or spending much of our children's growing years in Canada. I had been mildly concerned about them reaching adulthood and not feeling that they belonged anywhere. They were just babies yet, so far I had done no more than decide it was a decision I could put off. His words coalesced these vague thoughts into worries; however, they also had given me a course of action.

Very deliberately I compiled lists of Canadian holidays and how they were celebrated—Easter, July 1, Hallowe'en, birthdays, Christmas, Sunday dinner, vacations, etc. Some customs were special to my husband's family and some to mine and some were more generalized Canadian traditions. The resulting mix that has evolved over that last two decades is an amalgam not entirely Canadian but they are most specially *our* family traditions.

For example, on Hallowe'en we always have two pumpkins of some kind and each child always carves out their own design; and we always have a real Christmas tree whether it is spruce, cedar, pine or banana. We also have a tattered old tablecloth called the "birthday cloth" for family birthday meals and always watch family slides on Christmas Eve after the tree is lit. Each little ritual has its own special story that gets repeated over and over again.

Now that the children are leaving home and it is becoming harder and harder to find time for family activities, I had thought of abandoning some of these expensive and time-consuming celebrations. In nearly 20 years there had not been a hint that anything I had so conscientiously planned was making any difference—until last Saturday.

Perhaps it is not until they leave home that these family traditions become important to our children. Perhaps when they establish their own families some of the pride and love I tried to express through these special times will be passed along to another generation. That will be reward enough.

Soda Bombs and Soup Mix

Ottawa, October, 1988

Protocol. Precedent. Panic. Whatever the reason, one of the de rigueur preliminaries to a diplomatic posting used to be "the letters". Maybe it still is. These were the epistles to the wife of the Head of Mission and the letters of questions that were directed at one's predecessor. Both were written in hope. The former in hope that it elicited a short warm response and the latter in hope that it would unravel some of the mystery surrounding the posting ahead.

It was expected that the outward bound wife would introduce herself via a graceful handwritten note to the wife of the Head of Mission, expressing eagerness to become a member of the mission, pleasure at serving under her and her husband and indicating by an appropriate turn of phrase, one's suitability for the role of diplomatic wife. It was also the custom to include in this letter an offer of assistance. This offer was two pronged. One was an inquiry as to whether there were any small items for which she had been pining. Of course, if there were, it was a moral and social obligation to find them and hand carry them to post so that she need pine no longer.

The second line of Helpful Hurriedness was to offer to arrange for, or ship along with one's personal goods, items for the Canadian stall at any of the yearly bazaars. There do not seem to be as many of these international fêtes as there once were but at one time they were the scourge of diplomatic life. One could be sure that over the year there would be several of these affairs to organize. The offer to bring out the necessary cases of Canadian salmon and maple syrup would be sure to instantly ingratiate a new arrival into the good graces of the senior wives. It proved one knew how to do one's share, hold up one's end, wave the flag, carry one's weight and not let the side down. Try to do those all at once and not sweat while doing it!

Procuring these items could often be a protracted and thankless task. It is a myth that any company, retail store or craft outlet will jump at the chance to donate items to these affairs. If not as an outright gift for the glory of being associated with the diplomatic life, then at least to ask only cost price. Ottawa is not a large city. The number of outlets that can be tapped by the missions abroad is limited. The successful search for a flattered first time donor requires ingenuity, tenacity and connections.

Details of individual international fairs blur in memory, thanks be, but on one occasion it had been decided that Canadian (well, North American, at least) cosmetics would be hot ticket items at one such tropical event. It may have been a decision based on connections rather than common sense as it turned out. Anyway, boxes of lipstick and powder, moisturizer and nail polish arrived. Such beautiful shades. Pearly Pink, Blushing Coral, Misty Mauve, Barely Beige. On the day of the bazaar it finally dawned on the Canadian contingent that lipstick melts in 45 degree Celsius temperatures and pink blush does not complement a dark complexion. Ingenuity to the rescue. Put the lipstick in ice buckets and flog the blush and foundation to colour compatible embassies.

On another occasion, only three out of ten cases of salmon destined for the bazaar had cleared customs. These were the large one pound tins, not the easy to use up minis. Three days before the bazaar, tins of Pacific salmon appeared at a local market stall frequented by diplomatic shoppers and at less cost than we were asking at the fair. Our tins stayed on the plastic maple leaf decorated table. Another little tradition reared its head about that time; members of the mission were expected to purchase unsold items, especially junior members. Needless to say, I was very junior at the time. This was probably so that the senior wives would not have to acknowledge that "their" items had not sold well. As a result, salmon quiche and salmon tarts and salmon sandwiches and salmon mousse were staples at Embassy events for months after the bazaar.

The other dreaded curse that lurked around the edges of an international bazaar was the request for a "cultural event". The sight of three stout wives in dirndl skirts and peasant blouses clogging away at centre stage can send tremors down the spine of the staunchest patriot. You see, when the Brits decide to render a Scottish fling, there is nothing left for the Canadians but the Ottawa Valley clog.

Easier to write but equally fraught with danger is the letter to ones predecessor. To ask a stranger to advise on market deficiencies, the quality of hairdressers, the availability of children's books and the suitability of domestic staff is as reliable as consulting a Ouija board.

Personal priorities and preferences are barely understood in a long term relationship let alone between strangers.

Bring dry soup mixes. Spritzer bottles are a must, bring lots of soda bombs. There are no shoes to be bought here. You will need all your children's underwear for three years. Bring toilet paper. Bring Pampers. Bring Christmas cards. Bring, bring, bring. Buy. Buy. Buy. The Visa and MasterCard companies rub their hands in delight. My cynical advice is, if the local market does not offer it, learn to do without. That being said, there are posts where the local market is so sparse that nearly all one's groceries and necessities must be brought in from a convenient international distributor.

Never mind. Three years later you can ship it all back home again. In some dark corner of our basement there still lie six dozen soda bombs from a posting to New Delhi a quarter of a century ago.

Life in the Servant Belt

Ottawa, May, 1989

Twenty years ago, fresh and relaxed after an exhilarating thirty-six hour flight from Gander to New Delhi with two children under two, I deplaned into the searing Indian sunshine to be greeted by the High Commissioner and a full panoply of colleagues. It was our first posting. With more bravado than a brass monkey, I clutched my babies, shouldered diaper bags and strode into diplomatic life.

Initiation was swift and ruthless. Within twenty-four hours I had attended a lunch, a dinner and two receptions. I had viewed my new home and experienced an Indian marketplace. I had been introduced and briefed. All of which left me certain that, if I were to survive, it was imperative that I hire competent domestic staff as soon as possible.

Easier said than done.

The first set that I accepted on the recommendation of a bachelor turned out to be a bad choice for a family. The second set came from a colleague whose government authorized very generous pay scales for domestic staff, a choice which was not satisfactory to the applicants after I explained my pay scale. The third set came from differing castes, language and religious backgrounds, a bad choice for domestic harmony. The fourth set came from referrals from the most important person in the house, the children's ayah, whom I had hired on the recommendation of another Canadian mother for whom she had worked. They stayed with us for three years.

During the intervening years, the foibles and ingenuity of assorted domestic staff have generated much laughter and many tears. In the end they were more important to the outcome of the posting than the ambassador, even after my husband became the ambassador.

Many situations were generated out of my ignorance compounded by their ingenuity. Seemingly innocent requests can be loaded with implications.

Such was the case when the Indian dhobi, laundryman, asked whether he should do my laundry as well as Sahib's. To my mind it was a frivolous question. Why should he be paid to do laundry and leave half of it undone?

What I did not realize was that there was laundry and there was laundry. In India, shirts, blouses, slacks and cotton everyday dresses could be done by the hired dhobi; only a female full time servant would be allowed to do Memsahib's personal laundry, that is, my underwear. My male dhobi had end run the tradition. To prove his privileged status to the world my Mark's and Spencer's cut-for-comfort cottons and Sahib's sturdy Stanfield's graced the front lawn every laundry day for three years. The lacier ones he hung to dry on a special bush. These I successfully removed from his purview by washing them myself on his days off. I tried repeatedly to remove the others to the rear yard but he remained adamant that the sun was better in the front garden. This in a country where the sun shines back and front twelve hours a day every day of the year.

On another occasion and in another country I tried to instill the concept of the compost heap into the gardener. Over several months, compostable garbage and yard sweepings went into a pit and were nurtured with attention. As another planting season approached I looked forward to returning to nature that which was nature's. On an auspicious morning I instructed the gardener to "look after" the compost. I demonstrated turning it over, aerating it, because tomorrow we would begin the planting of the garden.

I returned home to the aroma of burning vegetation. Every scrap of compost had been carefully burned to make room for the additional compost which would be generated during this growing season. I will never know what he thought I was doing with the compost—some sort of peculiar plant worship, I suppose. He thanked me for the tip of opening it up so the air would help it burn so much better. He put the ashes on the garden which, indeed, did flourish. This was the same gardener who ran a sideline in selling extra vegetables to other people who sold them on the street. "His" garden consisted of the thinnings I had insisted he remove to allow the remaining crop of beets, chard and carrots to grow to full size. It took me several weeks to learn where his garden was located—he planted the thinnings in between the rows of "my" garden. Applaud ingenuity or pull them out? I left them be; I would have more chard than we could eat anyway. I did learn one gardening fact though; transplanted carrot thinnings grow into wonky multi-legged trolls.

Status symbols are another tricky area of mutual incomprehension. Consider the time the house sweeper requested to wash the car. It was dirty so I agreed. Over the next few days I slowly realized that the household was not running smoothly. The cook was surly, the bearer was uncooperative and the gardener was skulking behind the garage. Unknowingly, I had granted a status privilege to a low status servant and everyone's nose was out of joint except the sweeper's, and he was busy preening himself in the car mirror.

There is a popular belief among the uninitiated that the presence of servants makes representation a breeze. Dinner parties bring out the best and the worst in one's staff, especially in cultures where the word "No" does not exist.

"Do you know how to make Charlotte Rousse?"

"Yes."

"Is there enough rice to make pulao for twenty people?"

"Yes."

"Do you understand?"

"Yes."

"Do you need someone else to help you prepare for the party?"

"It is up to you, Memsahib." Means both yes and no simultaneously and may be interpreted, "I'll sulk if you do because it means you think I can't do the job and I'll sulk if you don't because it is too much work."

Deciphering recommendations are another treacherous aspect of managing domestic staff—not for what is written but for what is not written. Characteristics and qualifications not stated can be presumed not to exist, for example, "Esperanza follows instructions well" means she has to be told very explicitly what to do otherwise it will not be done; "Vladimir always arrives on time and has several dishes at which he excels" means he is sent by the state and knows two recipes. On the other hand, "Mustapha is intelligent, hard-working and honest" probably means just that.

If you are fortunate, there will be a very special employee who comes into your life and without whom your life would be less than it is. I was fortunate because such a person crossed my path early in my foreign service life. I am referring to my children's nanny, their "ayah" as they are called in India.

She became both mother and mentor to me and my infant sons during a very critical period. She eased my transition from merchant's daughter to diplomat's wife and started my children along the path to becoming the fine young men they are today. Today she lives in Canada and is part of their lives still. A fortuitous happenstance of the erratic assignment process for which I am very grateful.

As I wait through the vagaries of another assignment process, and contemplate another tour in the "servant belt", I remind myself that it is easy to have a laugh at the expense of one's domestic staff but it is wise to remember that these are the people who know more about you than your mother. They can make your posting a delight or a misery.

CENTRAL AMERICA : 1989-1992

Costa Rica, El Salvador, Guatemala, Honduras, Nicaragua, Panama

After seven years at home in Ottawa, DFAIT offered us another overseas assignment, this time to Central America. Not a region with which we were familiar except in a general way but one in which the Minister of Foreign Affairs and International Trade, the Right Honourable Joe Clark, was deeply interested. And so, we accepted.

At this time, the region was a mess: full scale insurgency was being fought in El Salvador; the United States was backing insurgency in Nicaragua; Manuel Noriega, Panamanian strongman, was tweaking the American tail; Guatemalan military was raining destruction on the native people; Costa Rica and Honduras were being dragged into the wars being waged on their borders. In order to join in actively seeking to end these wars, the Canadian government under Prime Minister Brian Mulroney became a member of the Organization of American States. For the next three years, the job of the Canadian Ambassador in Central America was to be point man for Canadian efforts in the peace process. Key to this peace initiative was the formation of ONUCA, the United Nations Observer Group in Central America, one of the UN's most complex and successful interventions.

In 1989, the United Nations became directly involved in peacekeeping and peacemaking efforts in Central America when the Governments of Costa Rica, El Salvador, Guatemala, Honduras and Nicaragua requested its assistance in the implementation of their collective agreement—the Procedure for the Establishment of a Firm and Lasting Peace in Central America, known both as the Esquipulas II Agreement and the Guatemala Procedure.

The creation of ONUCA signaled the arrival of an international consensus on efforts to bring to an end the wars in El Salvador and Nicaragua and the associated destabilizing presence of the United States' supported Contras in Honduras. Previous to this a large number of Canadian NGOs, non-governmental organizations, had put these wars at the centre of Canadian international concerns. The Honourable Joe Clark, Foreign Minister at the time, toured the region in 1987 and saw a role for Canada in the peace efforts. The Central American governments were attempting to isolate the United States from their own peace efforts which provided conditions that, for the first time in a decade, gave real hope to the peoples of the region.

Canada spearheaded the ONUCA group and in November, 1989, a small group of Canadian military arrived in Tegucigalpa, the capital of Honduras. The initial group was headed by General Ian Douglas, a hard-nosed experienced paratrooper, who understood that effective leadership is always from the front. He was replaced by General Lewis MacKenzie, a politically astute general who ably completed the mandate. Serendipitous choices or not these two men were perfect bookends for the mission, one a vigourous, get-it-done opening salvo and the other a tactful consensus building closer.

The Canadian group was an ad hoc one, having been cobbled together from disparate commands across Canada. For many of the men, their first contact with each other was on the plane to Central America. The Canadian Ambassador to the region, Gar Pardy, and Peter Boehm, the embassy's political officer, were in Honduras to welcome the Canadians and begin their political introduction to the complexities of the region. A private room in the best restaurant in Tegucigalpa, Azulejos at the Hotel Real Internationale, was reserved and for six hours, fortified by good food and Honduran beer, diplomats and soldiers discussed the personalities, politics and persuasions of the region.

By January of 1992, the process was essentially complete and ONUCA's mandate was considered completed and it was disbanded: the Contras had been integrated into Nicaragua's political system and democratic elections had been held; the insurgency in El Salvador had ended and plans for democratic elections were under way; Honduras was freed from the presence of the Contras and an international consortium had been established to coordinate relief and development efforts in the region. The Americans had removed Manuel Noriega from Panama and democratic elections had been held.

These efforts toward peace consumed most of our time in Central America.

United Nations peacekeeping operations have not had a particularly successful history. The failures have had more prominence than those that made significant contributions to peace. ONUCA did make a difference. Today it is difficult to find news about Central America in the mainstream media. For the record, however, it is worth noting that Oscar Arias, the spark that flamed into a peace process in the late 1980s, is again President of Costa Rica. Equally, Daniel Ortega, voted out of office in Nicaragua's first democratic elections in 1990, was re-elected in 2006 as that country's President.

Plus ça change...

A Long Day's Journey into Tomorrow

In 1990, I was in Nicaragua for the elections. Democratic elections to choose between the head of the Sandinista National Liberation Front (Frente Sandinista de Liberación Nacional or FSLN) and current president, Daniel Ortega, and head of the National Opposition Union (Unión Nacional Opositora, UNO), Violeta Barrios de Chomorro.

In the tense days before the election, random travel about Nicaragua was not to be taken casually, however, a small convoy of diplomatic cars was likely to be treated well as long as we were not poking our noses into sensitive places, asking too many questions and not going about after dark. By us, I mean the non-official embassy persons, i.e., us wives.

Canada was well regarded in Central America. Most of us speak Spanish, don't flash jewellery or cameras and are genuinely interested in the people we meet. Our main interest is in talking to the ordinary people, the market sellers, the restaurant servers, the old men sitting in the sun at the farmer's market. The official personnel are off talking with official people and we wander about the streets and villages. I wanted to test the street polls for myself. We visited León, Masaya, and Granada and attended the final Sandinista rally in Managua. It was intense, exciting and, ultimately, validation for the ONUCA presence.

Despite a broken leg, Violeta Barrios de Chomorro wins the 1990 election and remains in office until 1997. She turns out to be a charming lady of intellect and firm views.

Managua, Nicaragua, 1990

On the way to León is the barrio of Ciudad Sandina. Many families here have opened their homes to orphans of the fighting but one woman is doing something very special. In a dilapidated, poorly lit house, a few dozen orphans are being taught to paint the little wooden plaques with the quaint typical scenes that tourists love to buy. Doña Blanca is a small, quiet person who never raises her voice to the children. They come after breakfast when they can. Sometimes the older ones have to go out to work but the young ones come nearly every day.

The plaques are bought by a government distributor and the children receive some money for producing them. The plaques are painted in the brilliant primary colours of car body paint; there are so few cars to repaint that the cans of existing paint can be had cheaply. Several of the children are very talented and also create oil paintings of naive poignancy. These paintings are sold directly from this "studio" and all of the money goes to the young artist. More than money, these children receive love, attention and consistency, something their young lives have rarely known.

The sturdy stone walls of León are pockmarked with bullet holes from the Sandinista revolution and the cathedral clock still marks the hour that the Samoza bombs fell. Outside the cathedral, a few people sell home crafts and sour oranges while two small boys play tag among the pews. One of them cut his foot on a piece of garbage and nonchalantly washed it off in the filthy gutter and tied a dirty rag around it. Farther down the street, three teen-aged soldiers with automatic weapons watch an old woman sweep the street and a girl child fill a bucket of water from the public fountain.

In another direction lies Masaya, the artisan centre. Masaya is not a beautiful town, not even a quaint one. It is old, shabby and splotched with political graffiti. In fact, political graffiti has been painted onto every flat surface in all of the towns and villages. There will be no way to remove it except to paint it over which might not be a bad thing. The buildings all need painting and the people need to start healing their differences.

Outside the market, undernourished ponies wait patiently in their shafts for the next client wanting a taxi carriage. Inside the market, painted plaques and crude leather goods, typical paintings and wooden goblets attract more flies than tourists. There are some creative soapstone carvings but most attractive are the colourful sisal mats.

At the edge of town, women working in a small open air factory card, twist and dye the tough sisal rope. The carding machine is made of rows of rusty spikes pounded into a hand-hewn timber and the spinning wheel is counter weighted with stones and scrap metal. The little girl hanging up the dyed skeins is too short to reach the wire line but she tosses them over with practiced accuracy. In a room with two tables and space to stand, a woman and boy are hand stitching the sisal into traditionally patterned mats.

She tells me it takes her about four days to complete a three by five foot mat because the sisal cuts her fingers so she cannot work more than a few hours a day. I asked her how much she would make from such a mat but she just shrugs; her boss is leaning over the window frame listening to our conversation. She never once takes her eyes off the mat or stops working.

Beyond Masaya is the beautiful lakeside town of Granada. In the park tall, graceful royal palms sway against the blue sky. In front of the church, a fine black funeral wagon drawn by matched horses, decorated with flowers and black net, waits in solemn ceremony. Granada does not seem to have as much political graffiti and some of the buildings are freshly painted. In fact, there must have been a sale of shocking pink and turquoise paint because in one street nearly every building sports doors, balconies and entrances in these colours.

There are several hundred small islets around the edge of Lake Nicaragua, each one inhabited by one family. We rent a launch and spend an hour amid the peaceful channels and water lilies watching the storks and pelicans catch fish. From the rocks old men toss round hand knotted fishnets into the water and for some minutes I watch two young boys tend two fishing cormorants. The young man driving our launch has his home on one of these islets as had his father and grandfather. All the property is hereditary and cannot belong to anyone except these families. The inhabitants, who live independently of the municipal electrical and water supply systems, who go to market by water instead of road and who harvest the lake for food and income seem more fortunate than the campesinos who have had to flee their small farms and trust to the beneficence of the capital city, Managua.

In Managua, nothing has been rebuilt since the centre of the city was flattened by the 1972 earthquake. The designated international funds did a Samoza sidestep. There is no city centre, no downtown. There are various sections with a few stores, houses and restaurants but there is no commercial centre. There is no need for one because there is no significant merchant class. A few large nationalized agro-industries produce export crops but there is very little opportunity for entrepreneurs. One open-air cement block factory with half-a-dozen workers is operating along the road to León and somewhere there must be a factory for kapok mattresses because stacks of these brightly-coloured mattresses are common along the streets of Managua.

Managua probably has more parkland than any other city in the world. This is not by design but because leveling the earthquake rubble and covering it over is the only affordable way to clean up the city. Acres of flat construction sites await their opportunity. In the meantime, they provide pasturage for small wandering herds of cattle. The standing ruins shelter the homeless or house nesting birds. The lake which could provide water, food and recreation is polluted by raw sewage beyond any use. It is completely ignored by everyone. In what had been the commercial centre of the city, the soaring skeleton of the Basilica stands in mute reminder of other days. A gang of boys has made it their clubhouse and they perch on the high stone arches, silently remote from the activity on the streets below.

José sells old cigarettes while his mother sweeps the street around a municipal parking lot. On the streets people ride in battered, smoke-spewing antiques or, more commonly, on benches in slat-sided trucks. Roadsides are littered with burnt-out and abandoned car bodies and most vehicles are miracles of ingenious reparations. In the parking lot are twenty-four brightly painted new buses. After thinking it over, I conclude that these buses are for tomorrow's elections, to bring Sandinista voters to the polls and rallies, their shiny newness a not so subtle symbol of political power and wealth.

Next to the parking lot is the small concrete Plaza de la Cultura where, in a unique display of togetherness, are flying both the red and black banners of the Sandinistas and the blue and white banners of the UNO, the main opposition party. Nearby is located La Plaza de la Revolutión, a huge open field with a grandstand, where a quarter million supporters will gather for the final Sandinista rally.

The next day, the day of the rally, I go to the Canadian consulate which abuts these two plazas to form a triangle. It is about seven in the morning of a clear, hot day. First to arrive are the women and children with their charcoal braziers and round-bottomed pans for cooking rice and beans, fried bananas and pork. The children decant soft drinks and beers into plastic bags to be sold to the thirsty crowds. There are few men at this hour. They arrive later, brought in by truck. Most of the men wear clothing advertising the Sandinista party. The clothing is provided free by the party. Full political dress is a white Ortega T-shirt, a baseball cap in red or black with appropriate slogan, a red and black neckerchief and a red or white kami-kazi strip tied around the forehead or thigh.

In casual contest with the official party, I decide to test my political polling skills. They have more or less decided that the entrenched Ortega forces will triumph over the ONA upstarts led by Violeta Chomorro. I do not have courage enough to taste the greasy food, even after the flies are shooed away but the women talk with me anyway. One of the women says her daughter has a good job and is earning twenty dollars a month; one bragged of a son-in-law earning sixty dollars a month. They all shrug their shoulders over the economic and civil conditions and have no plans beyond tomorrow. These strata of society, which is most of the civilian population, exist in a nearly cashless economy. One man opines that attendance at the rally is more practical than political, a small price to pay for a free T-shirt, an afternoon of dancing and lemonade. Two days later, it turns out he is right. Violeta Chomorro wins. Three cheers for the secret ballot.

The rally starts in mid-afternoon with a raucous stage show to entertain people as they stream down the central street into the plaza. The field itself is masterfully managed with long lines of young men placed around the plaza to separate large groups and give the appearance of huge numbers. The crowd responds obediently to calls for flag waving and cheering. It is well-staged but not enthusiastic. Even the uninhibited lambada music inspires only a few modest hip swings throughout the crowd. At nine o'clock, after several hours of speeches and five minutes of fireworks, the crowds disperse in search of the trucks to take them back to their villages. I watch the fireworks from the terrace of a hillside restaurant; six hours of slogans, thirst, dust and heat is enough.

After a night of intense discussion between the parties and the mediation of the international observers, the votes are accepted by the losing party. Doña Violeta wins. Success. Political leadership is transferred after a democratic election. The ceremony is inexpert and marred by some instances of rowdyism but no one is killed. That's progress in Nicaragua. Today in Columbia, they shoot another political candidate.

The image of an old, dour-looking market woman comes to mind. I had spoken to her after the elections. Her grey hair indicated that she had survived a lot of history and I wondered if she had any insights to share. I had asked about her thoughts on life after the elections, would there be beneficial changes? After a few minutes she looked up and asked me if I wanted to buy some of her dried calabashes. When I shook my head in denial, she returned to contemplating the rooster tied up under her table. The look on her face was quite explicit—if I wasn't a customer, I was irrelevant, and a nuisance to boot. As a comment on foreign presence in Nicaragua, she may have had something to say after all.

It's a Small World

An article written for the Manor Park Chronicle, our community newspaper, after we departed on our first posting as Head of Mission, a euphemism in this case for His Excellency the Ambassador and Mrs. Not-Ambassador but who gets included as a social equal anyway.

Los Laureles, Costa Rica, November, 1989

Last summer a number of Manor Park families said good-bye to friends and neighbours and headed abroad to live for a few years. We were one of those families, not a complete family this time as we had to leave our children behind for the first time in twenty years. We had been able to remain together throughout their school years but they were grown up now and setting out on their own. They are thriving on their independence and so are we and so are the phone companies of Canada and Costa Rica.

In this land of sun and fun where it rains seven months of the year, there is no war, no famine and no army. And the rain only falls for a few hours, not all day. This is counterbalanced by daily sunshine whether it rains or not, roving potholes and people who use driving as a means of creative self-expression. Costa Rica is an oasis in a region of prickly factions, an ideal place to boogie off into the sunset for a time. Unless, of course, one works at the Canadian Embassy where they never seem to play a slow dance. This is not really Costa Rica's fault but if one lives on a busy block one can expect a lot of traffic. Canadian interest in Central America is high at the moment and we are well regarded by its countries making for a busy schedule as five of them are managed from here: Costa Rica itself, Panama, Honduras, El Salvador, Nicaragua as well as part of the responsibility for Guatemala. It means at least once, and sometimes three times a week, visits to other countries are required. Each of these necessitate landing and leaving from less than ideal airports in frequently windy, rainy, foggy conditions not to mention that most Central American airports are surrounded by mountains.

Fortunately for workaholics, there are eight days in the week here—in addition to the usual seven, there is also mañana. As it happens, this is also the most important day of the week because it is the day in which all the work is done, all the papers are signed and stamped, and the dry-cleaning is ready. This completely eliminates the need to agree upon completion dates; everyone always knows that it is mañana.

Escazú, where we live, is a hillside town contiguous with but semi-independent of the capital, San José. Our little suburb of a hundred or so houses has formed an association called the Los Laureles—because of the laurel trees not because of me—Residents' Association and we do battle with the municipality *jefes* to fill the potholes, put in lights, increase security, keep out throughways and improve traffic flow. Sound familiar? We do have one little problem not shared by Manor Park however—wandering bands of horses and cows which eat their way through the lawns and hedges and resist all efforts to drive them onto one's neighbour's greener turf. They are more likely to advance than retreat when I shoo them. I still walk the same dog, a large Newfoundland mix, and he retires from the field in their presence. Smart dog.

We spent one weekend admiring a newcomer's energetic efforts to renovate the front lawn and garden of an older house he had just bought. We were even amazed, but not surprised, at the speed with which seven wandering cows returned it to mud and stubble on Monday. Thus began the latest competition, the race of the wall-builders. Only the brave, or those with inedible gardens, are immune to the lure of concrete and wrought iron. Fantasy reigns supreme as pillared, arched, spiked and flower-boxed creations spring up around the block in defense of lawns and gardens. Ours, by the way, fills all of the four previous adjectival qualifications.

Yesterday I gave a speech about Canada, lauding its splendid seasonal scenery, vigorous climate and wild rivers. Today, as I admire my fruit-laden banana and mango trees and contemplate whether I will ask the gardener to pick oranges or papaya for breakfast, I admit there are compensations to life in the tropics. If only Costa Rica had crisp October mornings, gentle Christmas snowfalls, cheeky spring crocus, crunchy MacIntosh apples...

Coming, Looking and Going in the Darien Gap

One of my greatest pleasures at being the Ambassador's wife was the "chicken cheques". In countries where Canada is an aid donor, the embassy or high commission will be granted an amount of money called Mission Administered Funds, MAF money. These funds may be given at the discretion of the Head of Mission, the Ambassador or the High Commissioner, in pre-capped amounts to local initiatives. There are requirements to be met but, generally speaking, these are well spent funds. And they often go to women in relation to raising hens for food, eggs and profit, hence, "chicken cheques". Frequently, the money is to help build coops to prevent the birds from wandering, being beguiled away by neighbours or eaten by wild life or hungry roaming dogs. That the money raised from the hens usually goes to the women, not to their husbands, is an added bonus.

Central America abounded in such initiatives which provided many opportunities to give out the MAF cheques which meant meeting the recipients in small groups and learning at firsthand how the people live. Even at first hand however, what with being a diplomat, there is always that diplomatic barrier.

Panama, November, 1991

One of the periodic pleasures of being attached to the foreign service is the opportunity to visit out-of-the-way places. Without question, the tiny native settlement of Arimae in the southern region of the Darien province of Panama is out of the way. Arriving by road requires the simultaneous cooperation of the weather, the roads and the off-road vehicle; not to mention one's kidneys—bumps, ruts and energetic drivers shake one about. This is the Darien Gap, a terrain so formidable that linking the southern and northern legs of the Pan-American Highway has been impossible. The size of the mangrove swamp and the density of the jungle are so great that rooting out guerrillas and narco-traffickers has proven impossible. The most direct route is one hour by small plane to La Palma at the mouth of the Rio Sabanas; a long hour trip by outboard river canoe to Santa Fe; and then a half hour by jeep to Arimae. What from the air looks like tropical forest turns out to be jungle swamp with a few patches of solid ground supporting isolated huts and, rarely, villages of a dozen or fewer homes.

Travelling, fishing, transporting supplies and visiting are all done by dugout canoe. By the time the family, their goods, dogs and any stray passengers are loaded aboard, there might be only three inches of free board left. Needless to say, everyone sits very quietly as papa paddles along.

Being important guests, we are transported in a larger dugout canoe, with extended sideboards and outboard motor, which certainly makes it safer to cross the wide river mouth. Even so, any shifting to relieve cramped muscles provokes alarming rocking and increases the opportunities to be soaked by the bow wave. The impressiveness of one's arrival is determined by how elegantly one can clamber over the bow of the boat and scramble up the steep muddy bank without being covered in ooze and muck. The added obstacles of intervening canoes, slippery concrete slabs and helping hands only enhance the challenge.

Arimae is a ten-hut village with a school room, a street light to light the soccer field—there are no streets—and a canteen cum store which sells matches, oil, salt and soap. The electric generator is cranked up to run the street light for soccer games and town meetings. Even in this elevated area, after two days without rain, the ground is saturated with water. So much water and yet none to drink. Aqua-ducts and sanitation are top priorities. Homes are built in the traditional way on stilts with open sides and thatch roofs. Hammocks and the occasional hand-hewn table are the only furniture. Ancient school desks in the roofed meeting place are reserved for chiefs and male guests.

The purpose of our visit to Panama is to hand over a variety of Canada Fund cheques. Arimae is receiving a "chicken cheque", this time literally, a small sum which will buy hens and a rooster, build a coop and provide some instruction in poultry production. It is traditional for the women to have scratch hens about the village and the ones we see look fat and succulent from feeding on the grains of rice that fall to the ground from the husking mortars. However, the need for increased protein in their diet is apparent in the red hair and pot bellies among the toddlers.

Very wisely, the village had not made any arrangements in honour of the occasion as it would have been unseemly to second guess the fates by assuming that we would actually arrive. The gods were right, partly so anyway. The local Catholic Bishop, who was to accept a cheque in support of an aquaduct at the same time as the chicken cheques were to be given out had gone to a different village in the other direction whence it would take over an hour to fetch him. So, leaving the men to socialize as they wait for someone to find the village *jefe* who had also disappeared about his business and collect everyone for the ceremony, I go for a look about. I meet two memorable people.

The first is a lone woman pounding rice with a double-ended pestle in a wooden waist-high mortar. I heft the pestle. It weighs several kilos. I admire the dexterity with which she removes the husk and avoids breaking the grains. She speaks a little Spanish and we try conversing. We each agree that children are a worry to raise, housework is never done and husbands are always hungry. Then she asks a few pertinent questions of her own; who am I (unimpressed), why was I there (pointed to the fat hens about her feet), how long was I staying (relieved that I wouldn't have to be fed with one of her hens). Throughout the conversation she never misses a stroke with the pestle nor loses a grain of rice to the mooching hens; a lady with her priorities firmly in place. In an insightful twist on an old saying, she sums our visit all up by commenting, "You're coming and looking and going."

The second is the village chief. Under pressure from the boatman, who foretells dire consequences if we miss the tide, and the Ambassador who paces about consulting his watch, it had been decided to proceed with the ceremony without the chief. The ambassador does not want to spend the night! On the way in we had seen that the only accommodation is a corrugated steel lean to at the edge of the swamp! Ten minutes into the speeches, the chief arrives.

Barefoot, sweaty from the fields, with raggedy pants and torn T-shirt he could give lessons in aplomb and grace to any seasoned diplomat. Without a twitch or stammer, he greeted the crowd, unhurriedly shook hands in order of protocol, welcomed the guests and granted permission to proceed with the ceremony.

When the Bishop arrives another ten minutes later, and expresses some confusion over "our" chicken project as he is also discussing a chicken project for the village, the chief points out that, as chief, his responsibility is to get chicken into the stomachs of his village. Through

INCADI, a Panamanian NGO, he has chosen the Canada Fund as the most direct method of achieving this goal. For those readers who may spy a potential for conflict between the regional development interests of the church and a local NGO, that is not the case. Neither the Bishop nor the NGO were distressed and immediately set about deciding how to coordinate their efforts on this and other projects.

During the resulting period of discussion and clarification, the chief stands quietly with our cheque firmly in hand, a gentleman with his priorities firmly in place and a striking symbol of the new reality in developmental assistance. A reality in which the recipient firstly expresses choice and, secondly, appreciation.

A chicken cheque will not save the world but, if among all the coming and looking and going some learning also takes place, there will be more chicken in the pots and fewer pots on the children.

Ministerial Mischief

San José, Costa Rica, May, 1991

Diplomats are a puckish lot. That may explain why, from time to time, one feels like taking a hockey stick to them and executing a firm slap shot up centre ice. If we feel that way toward each other, imagine what the host country feels when en groupe the dip corps shoots its cuffs and starts stamping its Florsheims.

We had been inadvertently embroiled in a little toe-stomping foot-stamping brouhaha a few months ago. It came about innocently enough through the random merging of unrelated events.

The first move was made when a prominent southern neighbour reached down into its candidate bag and appointed an enthusiastic Ambassadress whose dedication to duty was seconded only by her predilection for lavish hats and stiletto heels. Armed with only a wide brim and a pair of Bally stilettos, she charmingly cut swathes through the densest gatherings. Unfortunately, she had the tiniest tendency to overreact which manifested itself in an incredible ability to paint herself into a corner.

She and our present Ambassador, my husband, presented their credentials on the same day and a special camaraderie exists between them, formed during the tense moments in the waiting room. A relationship which is reinforced at all official and state occasions when, instead of consulting the Protocol Officer, the Ambassador merely seeks out the most elaborate hat and slots behind it as the order of precedence is determined by the order in which one presents credentials.

The next connection with the incident in question was forged when our Ambassador decided to take the evening-before plane instead of the following before-dawn one and sent the chargé to the quarterly gathering of Heads of Mission in his place. As a result, our Ambassador in absentia became the North American regional dip corps representative to the Costa Rican government. Thus, in any dip donnybrook our Ambassador would be expected to step forth and staunchly defend regional honour and seek accommodation with the Costa Rican government.

The final piece was moved into place when the newly elected Costa Rican Minister of Transport precipitously acted to fulfill a campaign promise. Spurred on by criticism in the press of government inaction, he decided that his ministry at least would make a show of strength that the public could not ignore. The notorious streets of San José would be unclogged and traffic would flow unimpeded. Almost overnight the traffic police were expanded and the master plans set in motion. Never mind that it had taken decades for the roads to build up to the present level of congestion, confusion and chaos, with one fell swoop all would be solved.

And so, between Sunday sundown and Monday sunup the rules changed and customary driving habits verboten. The rules in question were those governing restricted parking on city streets which were universally ignored.

The traffic police had a field day. Street vendors were sent packing, their licenses checked, the size of their carts measured, their right to block the busiest streets reneged. Delivery trucks were given tickets for unloading goods after nine o'clock on proscribed streets, several blocks of the city core became pedestrian malls and on-street parking banned.

There were so many cars to tow away that extra help had to be called on and supplementary depots created to hold the towed vehicles. For the pedestrians it was the greatest spectacle of the year. They collected in brief groups, smiling and nudging each other as car owners looked helplessly at their disappearing car or searched the street in vain for their vehicle. The newly recruited police had been told that there were no exceptions and no excuses and they took this edict to heart.

Energized by the vision of having a Minister in charge of his domain, no one in the Ministry thought to tell the populace that Mr. Clean was about to descend on the city's plugged streets with a bottle of Liquid Plumber in his hand.

Thereby hangs the tale.

On this very same Monday the Ambassadress had an appointment with her milliner in the city centre on a block which had been declared "no parking"—and so, unknowingly she sailed unerringly into Dangerous Waters and grounded on a Diplomatic Incident.

Elated by the plethora of parking available, her driver pulled into an empty slot by the yellow curb on the strangely empty street and waited for the return of the Ambassadress. Not having ascertained the significance of an abundance of parking spaces, and accustomed to the magic protection of CD plates, he failed to realize that the defenses had been breached.

Asked by the police to remove his vehicle at once, he refused and quoted Diplomatic Privilege. The young *transitos* were unimpressed. After a brief, lively but unproductive discussion, the tow truck was called. When it became apparent that the car would be towed, the driver ran into the building to inform the Ambassadress.

The Ambassadress, the milliner and the driver rushed out of the building, leapt into the car, declared it part of a sovereign state and demanded to be put down. By this time the wheels were well and truly off the ground and about to come off altogether. Now we all know that Protocol and Privilege is a leaky boat in which to sail and, when tacking into the winds of affronted Local Authority, flying the Vienna Convention means diddly.

And so, grim faced but unbudging, the entourage was majestically towed across the city to a newly created impound lot where the car and its contents were sequestered pending payment of fines.

Hauling of the official car is one thing but, let me tell you, hauling the personage of the Ambassadress is a Serious Affront which calls for immediate Representations at the Highest Level.

By this time a dozen or so official diplomatic cars were residing at the impound lot. The ensuing consternation generated volatile internal rumblings and inflammatory outpourings of indignation. A movement was started to boycott the upcoming reception for the new Costa Rican president. Beware the Dip Corps when it decides To Do Something.

Amused rather than dismayed by the emotion surging around him, and never having fully taken on board the local language, our Ambassador was unmoved by the predicament. However, he was the elected regional representative and his duty was to soothe ruffled feathers and Resolve the Matter. The Ambassadress called, all her Latin colleagues called, friends of the corps called and fellow sufferers called. The Embassy switchboard crashed in exhaustion. Meetings were held with the Dean of the Corps and Official Calls were made on the Costa Rican Minister.

The most galling aspect of the whole thing for the dip corps was that for years they had been parking illegally all over town and getting away with it and wanted to continue to be allowed to do so. However, this hardly made a sound legal argument. The only defense that could be found was that the Corps had not been notified and, therefore, had not had an opportunity to comply with the new regulations (nor to negotiate special exemptions for themselves).

Face was saved, accommodation reached and apologies rendered all round. After a few months things returned to normal and dips resumed parking where they wished.

Talamanca South

Manzanillo, Costa Rica, 1992

The urge to go where no one has gone before is strong in us all. Short of descending into the ocean depths or ascending some geologic peak there are few places left on earth that meet that criteria. Anyhow, to go where only a few have gone before is enough for most of us.

The southeastern coast of Costa Rica might qualify for that description. Reached only by fair-weather roads through the banana plantations where Chiquita and Dole originate, by boat or by coastal footpath, the Manzanillo-Gandoca Biological Reserve is protected by its isolation and inaccessibility.

At the moment, those are the only things protecting it. The status of Reserve is a meager defense against developers, lumberers, poachers of wild fauna and flora, the immediate needs of a growing local population for land and the desire of bananeros to encourage every member of the ECC to consume daily the long yellow potassium-rich fruit.

The invisible agrochemical footprint of banana production is on my mind as I step down into the mud and wave at the barefoot children playing in the scummy green drainage stream.

For an hour we have been fishtailing in black gumbo through thousands of hectares of banana plants with their load of green bananas covered in the blue plastic bags which keep insects and the hairy tarantulas at bay. Beyond the plantations lies the coastal village of Gandoca and the Reserve. With a final slide and swoop the track ends abruptly in front of a cleared field with a weathered hut, safely raised on four legs above the water-logged earth.

"Hola la casa! Buenos dias, señora. ¿Por favor, diganos donde estamos?" "Where are we?" I shout to the woman hanging clothes to dry on the barbed wire fence of her garden patch. Her children clutch her colourful skirts in shy excitement at the appearance of strangers, foreign strangers.

"Aqui esta Gandoca, señores." This is Gandoca.

She has to be kidding. This is nowhere. It could not possibly be our destination.

The map had shown neat little black squares representing houses, a tiny cross for a church and a flag for a school. Where are they? There had been no little pigs, or coconuts, or wavy swamp lines on the map.

The guidebook had described a ranger station at the entrance to the reserve, a pleasant little village with a school, possible guides, fishermen who could be persuaded to take us along the coast and an unofficial hostelry where one could sleep sheltered for the night.

We look around. Two mud tracks intersecting in the middle of coastal jungle and banana groves, three huts on stilts and a roving band of hungry porkers grunting at the wheels of our Montero are not what we had expected. The wheels of our Montero are our immediate concern as they are hub-cap deep in marshmallow mud and inching toward the deep roadside ditch. People complain about winter driving in Canada but many times I have been thankful for the enforced practice with slippery conditions when faced with off-road tracks in the tropics. Rain and mud and river fords and potholes and sugar sand yield to the experienced hand and foot of wily winter drivers.

A few anxious moments later, safely parked with two wheels on a grassy hummock, we look around. Despair turns to elation upon discovering that we are only a kilometre from the beach and the reserve entrance is just around the corner. The peace and quiet gradually penetrate the adrenalin fog and we make ready for the trek to the beach. Sun hats, high gum boots and water bottles for everyone. One camera and a pair of binoculars between us will suffice; it is too hot to lug more. It is well over thirty degrees Celsius with the humidity approaching one hundred per cent. The entrance to the Gandoca-Manzanillo Biological Reserve is marked by a few wooden fence posts, a small carved sign and an empty hut. The trail would have been drivable in the dry season but now it is impassable, even to horses, because of the mud.

How do the people keep their homes clean, or dry their laundry? Where do they shop? They need rice and beans, coffee and sugar. How do the children get to school? Only for the first few years can they attend the local school, a freshly painted hut on stilts in the middle of a cleared quarter acre. Turquoise seems a popular colour. There are a number of turquoise doors and window frames but the school, being more important, is all turquoise. There are no children above the age of ten so the rest must hike out to the main road, several kilometres away to pick up the school bus.

Bright turquoise does not stand out here, where blood-red and scarlet heliconias grow in ranks several metres tall along the forest edge. Jewel-like colours punctuate the jungle greens from every nook and cranny. One would assume that emerald green and crimson birds would be easy to spot but a shy Slaty-tailed Trogon sitting quietly on a branch is nearly invisible until it flies.

"Look at the purple flowers on that tree," someone calls out. "That's not the tree; it's a vine growing on the tree."

"Idiot, it's an orchid growing in the tree."

It's hard to tell where one plant starts and another begins. This time it is a vine, an escaped species of morning glory which thrives around domestic clearings. At home it is the vine of summer swings and front porches and Sunday dinner with Grandfather, here it is a weed.

Small yellow and black and orange and iridescent birds dart about the bushes. Blue and yellow and orange and black and red butterflies flirt with the flowers. They look too fragile to be so energetic in this wet heat.

In any event, we are more intent on rescuing our gum boots from the sucking mud and drawing air into our heaving lungs. For a year we have been living in the Central Valley at an altitude of 1,500 metres and are unaccustomed to the torrid sea level temperatures and suffocating humidity.

This land has been inhabited by bands of indigena, the native Indian people, for centuries. There are clearings for huts, small gardens, stands of coconut and banana and pastures for a few horses and cattle but still the jungle presses in. The indigena traditions emphasize harmony with nature and the preservation of a balance between human and environmental need. This is why we have come; to see how it was before it disappears under a wave of development opportunists and ecotourists. We ourselves are the forerunners of the very thing we deplore.

Suddenly, the land rises slightly and the trail opens onto the beach. It stretches away to the north and south for several kilometres, the sand pure black and powder fine, a reminder of Costa Rica's volcanic history. The slope is steep and the surf smashes and recedes, building and destroying transient sculptures of sand and driftwood and surging foam. It is wild, untamed and beautiful.

To the north, our left, stretches a long slow curve of beach fringed by coconut palms bending submissively in the wind. At first it seems that the place is empty but there are small houses in the trees, and gradually the signs of domesticity become obvious. There are clothes drying on fences, fishnets draped over upturned boats resting on the flotsam beached above the high tide mark, a few dogs sleeping in the shade and children playing on the stoops.

Our objective for the excursion lies to the south, the Gandoca Lagoon. It is a brackish mangrove-edged swamp, cut off from the sea by a ridge thrown up by the waves. During very high tides the sea rolls over the sand bar maintaining water levels and creating a protected, warm water haven for its resident populations. The Atlantic tarpon comes here to breed, a rhythm which the sport fishermen have thankfully ignored. There are caimans and seabirds and snakes, oysters and crabs, red mangrove and sea grape but we have come to see a rarer creature—the West Indian manatee.

The manatee is an ancient creature with small populations here and there around the world, in East Africa and northern Australia, Florida and South America. Referred to unflatteringly as the sea cow, it is also portrayed in legend as the siren of the seas whose seductive song can lure ships onto the rocks and sailors to their watery deaths, the dreaded lorelei.

Unfortunately, the manatee looks more like a cow with flippers and a stubby rudder. They are gentle vegetarians whose aim in life is to raise their young in peace while browsing contentedly among the sea grasses.

A few men and young boys walk past in small groups or alone. They smile and throw amused glances at the crazy gringos. The water in our bottles is hot and stale but we need it for the trek along the beach. In response to our request, one of the men scales a palm and cuts down a few young coconuts. He lops off one side with an efficient blow of his machete. The liquid inside is sweet, slightly bitter and tastes of coconut. It dribbles down our chins as we gulp it down. It is delicious. The flesh of the immature coconut is sweet and gelatinous, easy to digest in the steaming heat. We eat it by scooping out the jelly of the young fruit with a clean stick.

In this form it is called a "pipa" and the coconut is thrown away after the liquid has been drunk. The beaches are littered with them. These husks become home to an assortment of beach life, mainly crabs waiting out the sunshine hours between tides.

Heat waves shimmer in the noonday sun. The sand is too hot to touch and the surf too strong to walk in, besides the beach is too steep. We toil along the high tide mark, just out of reach of the snatching surf, slipping and staggering in the soft sand.

The sand barrier between ocean and lagoon is firmer and we shade our eyes against the glare as we search for our objective. The lagoon is glassy under the layer of hot air. Shorebirds dart in and out of the surf; fishing eagles and kingfishers glide among the mangrove trees; a lone fish skitters over the surface of the water to elude a feeding predator. There appear to be no snakes or caiman in the vicinity so we turn our attention to the ocean.

Nothing. Waves and more waves. Lunch is calling. Have we come this far to be foiled?

"Look. There. In the wave."

There are a thousand waves for goodness sake!

I see it. Brown, stubby, like a fat cigar rolling in the surf. Its back glides smoothly in a curving roll up and out of the water and down again. It is riding a roller. The tide is not at full flood yet so perhaps it is waiting to get into the lagoon for a feed. It may be tired of the endless surf and dreaming of the grassy bed in the sheltered lagoon, maybe anticipating a change of menu. Whatever it is doing, it does not do it again. That is the only sighting we have. The ten second reward for six hours of grueling effort.

It is enough.

The trip back to our campsite is relaxed and filled with hums of contentment. Tonight we will talk about what we have seen and done. For now, it is enough that we have done it.

Driving Habits

San José, Costa Rica, 1990

Dining out across cultures, working across cultures, dating across cultures. Among all the platitudes earnestly delivered over the years to prepare people for the shock of realizing that there is more than one way to do things, such as cook rice or raise children or make a pass or confront the boss, no one honed in on the obvious, driving across cultures. The fastest short course on the cultural differences between Canada and one's new country is a drive across town at rush hour, preferably on a rainy day with a national bike race about to begin.

The Canadian Embassy in peaceful Costa Rica is near as naught to ground zero San José, a place so relaxed that offices and businesses close for a two-hour lunch break. However, safely navigating the three kilometre drive from Paseo Colon to Calle 3 is a sweat-rousing hybrid between a Calgary chuck wagon race and a charge of Roman chariots. In the land of mañana they drive like there is no tomorrow.

This is not a form of aggression but an expression of the joy of life and an affirmation of its inconsistencies and surprises. Thus, when a two-way main street becomes one way, there is no indication of the change except the flow of the on-coming traffic. This also explains the lack of street addresses, road signs and lane markings; after all, the route markings along life's path are often obscure and ambiguous. Stopping to ask directions and have an extended discussion of the options is part of the journey.

Besides, too many rules and regulations would make it difficult to see and wave at friends and relations along the roadside. One's fervent hope when driving along a narrow lane is that the driver of the ice cream truck ahead of you is not a cousin of the driver of the approaching furniture van or you will be stuck for twenty minutes while they exchange family news.

Unannounced closings of major arteries do not indicate lack of planning, rather they express national pride and allow citizens to cheer runners or bicyclists or celebrate special days with street parades and fiestas. Also, the resultant congestion on the narrow seething side streets allows an unexpected pleasant opportunity to fulfill a driver's main obligation, blowing the horn.

At an intersection with a red light, for example, when the first driver in line toots his horn it may be to call the lottery ticket seller, emphasize a point to a fellow passenger or attract the attention of a pretty girl. The second and third drivers honk to let the first driver know that they are behind him and he had better look sharp when the light turns green. The last driver repeatedly honks to ensure that the light stays green until he clears the intersection. The car horn is merely an extension of the Tico, a local term for Costarican, love of social interplay and general gusto para la vida.

During the election campaign, horn-honking took on another responsibility. Partisans flew their party colours on long poles tied to the door handle inside so the flag could stick up much like a bicycle safety flag outside. When cars with the same flag passed each other, they honked in encouragement; when opposition cars passed, they honked in derision; when unmarked cars passed, they honked to spread the word. This made for an endless dialogue of significant tooting which terminated in twenty-four hours of celebratory/compensatory honking and tooting on the day of the election.

In most matters the Ticos are conservative and tradition-bound. For example, their favourite dish is rice and black beans. Now I love rice and beans, however, I also love variety. As an exercise in compromise and togetherness I planned several menus for the household around an assortment of rice and bean dishes. After a week the cook sadly informed me that all the books and recipes were in error about the preparation of rice and beans. In any case, there was only one way to make rice and beans so no other recipe was really necessary, thank you very much but here were my recipes back.

Costaricans are proud of their peaceful traditions and go to great pains to avoid confrontation, nationally and personally. Conflict is resolved by long, albeit sometimes loud, discussion. Hence, there is no army and no armed police force, although there are thousands of armed private security people as well as private citizens. A contractor will agree to every suggestion. A salesman will write up an order for a hundred square metres of blue tiles rather than upset you by telling you that there are none in stock. A colleague will accept an invitation even if she knows she will be in Miami that day. A repairman will agree to come on Thursday even when he means Monday. By Friday it will be too late for you to call another repairman and by Monday you will have cooled off and be grateful to see him.

Therefore, among a charming peace-loving people, apprehensive of change and adverse to confrontation, it is revealing that behind the wheel (of anything) they become risk-taking range-riding caballeros. Seatbelts and sobriety are an affront to self-esteem, signaling lane changes hinders self-expression and pedestrians and potholes defy the adage, close only counts in horse shoes.

Tico driving should not be viewed as reckless or irresponsible, rather as a joyful expression of faith in God, immortality and a continuous supply of rice and black beans. The motivating question is not, "Will I like it when I get there?" rather "Will I enjoy getting there?" An everyday omnipresent manifestation of their motto: *pura vida*, a phrase which expresses a philosophy that includes good spirits, enjoyment of life and a desire to celebrate their good fortune to be born Costaricense.

No Ivory Tower Here

San José, Costa Rica, April, 1992

It would be impossible to work at the Canadian Embassy in San José and not experience the flavour of Costa Rican life.

The Chancery is located in the heart of the city and our little corner is filled with vibrant, churning life. No other embassy is as well placed to feel the pulse of the city. A short time ago it seemed that Ottawa would follow the trend and move its embassy out to the suburbs in company with the Americans, the Japanese and the Germans. However, after several property scouting missions, budget restrictions forced a decision and building plans were scuttled. As a result, the Canadian Embassy remains one of a handful of diplomatic missions in the city centre.

[However, two years later, after a complete renovation including tile floors and new elevators, it was moved out to the suburbs. I reckon that Ottawa got nervous, decentralization reverted to centralization and three-quarters of the staff were downsized; one can have too much decision making at the post. But it was great while we were there.]

From the corner offices one can see into the treed Plaza de la Cultura with its artisan stalls, street hawkers and sidewalk painters. During the tourist season from November to May one can, in fact must, listen to the buskers and street entertainers who, on Friday, are assisted by very efficient loud speakers. The plaza is actually the roof of the underground Gold Museum and large tourist information centre. It is to here that we run when the earthquakes strike, feeling that it is safer to risk falling into the gold than be crushed by falling mortar.

On one corner of the plaza stands the Teatro Nacional with its austere exterior hiding the elaborate gold and green cherubs and curlicues of the interior. Another corner features the grand old Gran' Hotel de Costa Rica where sooner or later every tourist passes, not a few of which are Canadians requiring consular services.

Adjacent streets are lined with kiosks and barrows which sell fresh fruits, sunglasses, gaudy cosmetics and Hong Kong folding fans. Lottery ticket sellers vie for air space with juice venders and money changers. Acquiescing to the press of foot traffic, these narrow streets have been declared pedestrian malls.

The only exemption to this are delivery trucks and five embassy parking spaces. Since the street contains a major grocery store, a large book and office supply store, a restaurant and various small businesses, the main entrance to the embassy is an obstacle course of delivery trucks. The large front portico shelters pedestrians from the tropical showers who lure the lottery sellers into range of the guard's glowering stare and admonishing finger.

The three and a half block walk from the parking lot is an obstacle course of street life, potholes—not in the road, in the sidewalk—modern mothers and old winos, posh shops and urine splashed ruins, hustlers and pickpockets, executives and beggars.

If it were not necessary to brave the city core in order to park the car and walk to the office, very few would ever bother. I have heard many people in the diplomatic corps say they rarely go downtown and a few admit that they have never been downtown. What a shame! The new, pristine suburbs with paved boulevards, shopping centres and impartial privacy walls allow only a narrow, skewed view of Costa Rica. They create a seductive cocoon of comfort that anaesthetizes the mind and sucks away ones desire to break out and risk experiencing something new.

Many of the most memorable characters from this posting I have met within two blocks of the embassy door.

Two metres from the front entrance a middle-aged woman sits on a scruffy stool offering pot scrubbers made from twisted coconut fibre. She never asks for patronage, merely gestures at the meagre offerings. Sometimes she has a small baby on her lap. Whether or not it is hers, her daughter's or a stranger's, I do not know. Around the corner a man stands selling plastic coated wire hangers for Barbie doll clothes. He has obviously made these himself and hopes to cash in on Barbie's blond popularity which is as high here as at home. I have never seen anyone buy any of these items and the dispirited slump to their shoulders tells me that rarely do they.

Two corners north a young man peddles Tico fruit from a wooden barrow. Tico fruit is any indigenous fruit that foreigners are not likely to eat. The people of Costa Rica refer to themselves as Ticos and anything that they consider especially typical they also refer to as being Tico. My inquiries are usually met with a grunt and silent stare. After two years

I suspect he realizes that I am a fruit voyeur rather than a potential customer. From his wagon I have tried the musky *jocote*, the fragrant *marañon*, the furry, squishy *anono*.

To the west, a block and a half, a vender of home remedies displays his colourful selection of dried roots, leaves and barks. He offers palliatives and curatives for physical pain, mental turmoil and love-based lassitude. If you explain your symptoms, he will make you up a bundle to distil into water, or grind into powder. Their efficacy I have left untried but herbal remedies are an enduring tradition throughout the region.

The five blocks of the street mall alongside the embassy are patrolled by RCMP clones in straw sombreros painted navy blue and riding on bay horses. As Canadians we are accustomed to police on horseback but here they create a novel and unexpected sight. Most Ticos respond with chuckles and ribald comments. Unfortunately for the horses, the comments became more than ribald as pedestrians started stepping into horsie doo-doo and, thus, the horses now wear black leather sacs lined with garbage bags tied under their tails. Apparently nobody was interested in applying for an official pooper-scooper position and a different solution was necessary.

A final kudo and two heart tugs, all of which can be seen from the veranda of the Gran' Hotel de Costa Rica. As with the Long Bar in the Stanley Hotel in Nairobi, if one stays there long enough, eventually everybody you know, or want to know, will pass by.

From the veranda café one can catch a tour bus to every part of the country, have a haircut or shoes shined, buy souvenirs or a meal, listen to a marimba performance or simply watch the passing scene. Catching the eye of one of the cruising waiters to order a cup of spoon-melting coffee requires the determined application of charismatic finesse. Hence, a kudo. Rosita is short and plump with long black hair caught up in a huge bun and secured with red combs. From the far end of the veranda she can spot a regular customer and with a wave of the *cafetéra* let you know she will be there pronto. She never wastes a trip along the patio just to deliver one service; every trip delivers meals, takes orders, drops bills, clears tables and answers questions. She never seems to hurry but she never keeps you waiting. Her proficient attention and smile across the language barrier have become a familiar comfort.

Among the befuddled citizens of the street who mooch around this tourist mecca is an old man in a grey suit and bare feet. Years of abuse have all but wiped out awareness of his surroundings and grim reality is etched indelibly on his face. However, to the amusement of some and the tears of others, when the marimbas give their noontime concert, he dances and smiles to himself with the carefree grace of a young man out to win the heart of a beautiful Tica. His joy makes me smile and his reality makes me cry. I hope his memories are better than his present.

Whether on the way for a quick sandwich at the cafe of the Teatro Nacional or a languorous haircut and manicure at the barbershop, a detour to drop some coins into the hands of "The Old Lady on the Steps" is mandatory. Tiny, with white hair in thick braids on either side of a seamed brown face and a merry toothless smile, she resembles an ancient apple doll. Obviously poor, but clean and warmly dressed, she is deposited by her family in a sheltered corner of the veranda's side steps and reclaimed after lunch or when it turns cold or starts to rain. The fact that she is probably the richest mendicant in San José does not deter my instinct to comply with her gestured plea to drop a few coins into her palm. I figure the best way to ensure that she is cared for is to ensure that she remains her family's biggest asset. Who says you can't get by on your looks, even when you are eighty?

What Goes Around, Comes Around

Escazú, Costa Rica, 1992

My father dispensed wisdom via folk sayings. He seemed to have one for every occasion. "Round and round she goes and where she stops nobody knows." "If you're gonna dance, be sure you're willing to pay the fiddler." "What goes around, comes around". When I was younger I thought this last one meant that, if your friend had chicken pox, sooner or later, you were bound to get it, too. As the years went by, I realized there were broader interpretations. One such interpretation challenged me a few months ago.

At a clan gathering in the guise of an Embassy Coffee Morning which I was hosting at the Residence, discussion had turned, as it often does, to the difficulty of being a Diplomatic Spouse—family separation, lost jobs, elderly parents, adjustment trauma and posting anecdotes. By this time, I had advanced on my husband's coat tails to the heady status of Wife of the Head of Mission and I, perforce, was living in the Official Residence, referred to as the O.R. Hence, I cannot say, "a coffee morning at my home". I suppose I could have but it never felt that way.

At home or at the residence, it was a function I had performed dozens of times over the last thirty plus years.

Resigned to listening to the same old complaints created by a rotational career as expounded by a crop of recent arrivals, I nearly choked on my biscuit when one of the neophytes proclaimed with a sidelong look in my direction that, "Of course, it is different for the Older Wives. They never expected to Have a Career, and the Ambassador's Wife is Too Busy to Work anyway".

It was a tossup whether to laugh, cry or leap shrieking onto my chair. I was readying for the fray when the really sobering reality of the statement kicked my consciousness awake—the speaker unequivocally considered me an Older Wife. What had gone around, had come around. What's more, they thought the battle for departmental support for rotational spouses and families was their invention and nobody had ever railed against the world's injustices before; that those who preceded them were guilty of passive acceptance. Worse, the implication was that we Older Wives had not even seen the injustice.

Surprise! Did they think it was Treasury Board who decided that more family oriented Foreign Service Directives were needed? That the Under Secretary forced the Department to accept spousal employment as a valid issue? That the Department founded the Foreign Service Community Association?

The thought that stayed my hand and saved the Official-china-for-C-Posts cup and saucer from becoming airborne was the realization that I had been where they were and they would someday be here. I said a mental thank you to that forbearing Older Wife who had not thrown her cup at me in my brasher days of windmill tilting. So I opted for the devil's advocate role and settled down to find out what were the concerns of the new community members.

It should come as no surprise that there were actually no new concerns. The conversation could have occurred during any of a hundred mornings over the last quarter century. How discouraging. I had expected more of the Liberated and Politically Correct generation of Younger Spouses; more dynamism and less passivity; more constructive activity and less waiting for something to be done for them. During an ebb in the conversation, I realized what I had unconsciously been doing and another turn of the wheel came round. No longer interested in manning the barricades, I was endeavouring to prod the younger generation into activity, to nudge them into broadening personal gripes into more generic issues and to generate some practical solutions.

Had someone done this to me twenty-five years ago? Had I been the manipulated instead of the manipulator all these years?

The Foreign Service Community Association did not exist in those days. Instead, there was the External Affairs Officers Wives Association which had a loose, big sister arrangement that took all the Young Wives under their maternal wing and attempted to show by example How It Should Be Done. The name says it all. The dividing line was between those wives—and they were all wives—who, when on posting, would have to play an Official Representational Role and those who would not. The Officer's Wife.

While the employee posted abroad received a smattering of information related to the job, it was accepted that the accompanying dependents would be self-sufficient enough to ferret among the community for such support and information as they required when departing or returning to Canada. Self reliance and a sense of marital and patriotic duty was a highly prized attribute in those days and smiling, stiff lipped and silent acquiescence to the Exigencies of the Services was expected.

There were no pre-posting briefings, re-entry workshops or résumé writing seminars. These were not the issues that concerned the Older Wives when I was a Young Wife. The Foreign Service Community Association came later but, remember, it came at the instigation of these same Older Wives.

In my early years, it was whether or not the Younger Wives would be able to meet the demands of Representation and Protocol. In the early days, anyone becoming a Canadian diplomat came from the upper class—oh, yes, Canada had and has an upper class—but about the mid-sixties, entry was democratized and attendance at Upper Canada College was no a longer a prerequisite. Even the odd Newfoundlander could get accepted into the ranks. This meant that, tsk-tsk, their wives might not have attended Havergill or Bishop Strachan and, consequently, would probably not be familiar with the placement of crystal stemware in a formal table setting. The response to this Potential Situation was a series of coffees, luncheons, teas and, once before a posting, a dinner with the Divisional Head.

So it was that I left my infants in the care of an unknown babysitter, donned my best togs and assailed the stone fences of Rockcliffe Village for my first lunch lesson.

At the time, we were living in a third-floor walk up off Bank Street swamped in student loans and diapers, so I will admit that the stained glass double front doors and the wall-to-wall dove grey plush carpeting was a sharp reminder of my position. For an eon I sat on a satin sofa between two stalwart ladies from the Soviet Embassy—remember these were the days of Russophobia—who spoke as much English as I spoke whatever they spoke. Thank God the Protopopovs had just won Olympic gold. Every few minutes I could say "Protopopov" and smile. At the summons to partake of the buffet luncheon—first lesson, "luncheon", not "lunch"—I placed my crystal coupe d' imported on a silver coaster and sought the tail end of the line. I figured it was a safe bet that I should stand behind everyone else.

With discouragement I eyed the silver casserole holders, Wedgewood dishes and cut crystal stemware. How could I ever afford such things? Clearly, it was presumptuous to think that I could ever entertain Important People in Adequate Style.

Then I looked at the food on my plate and began to laugh. Tuna casserole! Despite the sterling silver fork, it was still only tuna casserole with canned peas. I had learned my lunch lesson alright, even though it may not have been the one intended.

Instead of fretting about the trimmings, I started to listen to the conversation—family separation, lost jobs, elderly parents, adjustment trauma and posting anecdotes. I listened and learned.

What goes around, comes around. A quarter century after the tuna casserole revelation, I found myself sitting in my Official Living Room as a Senior Wife dispensing wit and wisdom on the same old topics. I wonder if the Younger Spouses realized that only the quality of the tuna casserole is important?

Watch out for the Moose Now!

Gander, Newfoundland, 1992

In mid-May, the Newfoundland branch of the family gathered to bid farewell to one of its senior members and, thus, we abruptly left humid, fuggy, rainy Central America for the chilly, windy, not-quite-yet-Spring chill of Newfoundland.

"We're gonna head back now, afore it gits dark."

"Aw'right. We'll sees ya agin. T'anks fer cumin'."

"Still be light times we git to Dildo Run an' we leaves now. Some dark when t'sun goes down."

"Yis, bye. An' dere's moose on t'road. Feller saw t'ree t'uther marnin', up by Jake's Pond dey were."

"Some good t'eat, though."

"Yis, bye, dey is t'at. I'll git anuther one t'fall now. Las'one's all gone."

"Well, bye fer now."

"S'long. Watch out fer t'moose, now."

Everyone at the family gathering had a moose story and this final admonition was tagged on to every farewell. Moose in the yard, moose in the shopping center, moose strolling the TransCanada, moose looming in the car headlights and moose-car collisions; surely some of these were the same moose, there couldn't possibly be that many moose on the loose, even in Newfoundland.

Scepticism aside, there were 400 moose-car collisions last year. If half those moose were killed, they provided hospitals and government facilities in that province with 12,000 kilos of tasty, free meat. Hard on the cars, but good for the provincial budget.

Designed in a moment of silliness, a moose is an absurd creature. Its legs are too long for the heavy body, its magnificent shoulders taper to a scrawny rump and its majestic antlers spread their glory over a lugubrious, baggy-lipped face. However, never laugh at a moose. They have absolutely no sense of humour. After all, they don't laugh at us as we crack and snap our way around the spruce forest through which they manage to slip their 600 kilo bulk with wraithlike delicacy.

Absurd or not, they can be some impressive up close, as I have just had reason to experience.

During the aforementioned recent family gathering, in the midst of all the moose stories, it became obvious that I ("she's from t'mainland, ya know") had never seen a moose on the hoof. They made it quite clear that my Newfie husband was being shamefully remiss in his duties in not arranging for me to meet a moose. No time was to be lost. This was early Spring, the season for them to come out of the woods, and he was advised of all the likeliest venues for moose viewing, "down t'auld railway station", "out by Dead Men's Pond", or "up long Reachy Run".

We made the rounds. Not a moose.

The Sunday morning of our last day dawned with the spectacularly blue May skies and crystalline air that make a painter lust for his brushes. My lungs cried out for the rush that comes from such cold, pure northern air after months in the steamy tropics, so I went out for a walk.

The somnolent neighbourhood was still and silent. No children weaving along on little bikes with pink training wheels, or swinging shiny new bats at unscarred baseballs. The sun was glinting off the polished 4 x 4's and half-backs parked in the driveways. Here such vehicles are not macho machines for insecure yuppies but working vehicles. The ice was off the brooks and the salmon were expected to begin their dash up the rivers any day. What you can catch, trap or shoot, you don't have to buy so the vehicles were ready.

Reaching the end of the block, I turned back, to gaze at the modest, neat houses in their coats of bright paint and to ponder briefly on the road between then and now. With a sigh, I resumed my contemplative strolling, only to zoom back suddenly to reality as I found myself nose-to-nose with a three-quarter grown calf moose, puckering up for a nibble on my coat collar!!!

Surprise on both sides was total. Startled blue eyes stared into doleful brown ones. Too stunned to react, I stood motionless as he sniffed my buttons and whiffled a steamy greeting. Casually, he rejected me as either food or an enemy and ambled on down the pavement. I stood there until he vanished behind a neighbour's garage.

As they say on the Rock, "Lard Jayses, dey're some big."

"Nobody," I thought, "is going to believe me."

A few of the early-rising relatives had gathered for breakfast and I told them about my adventure. I could see their dubious looks. One of them asked me if I was sure it hadn't been a horse. Horses are rarer than moose in Newfoundland so I scoffed at that riposte.

I pointed out the window to amplify the tale and there, ten feet from the back window, was another moose. A full-grown cow moose this time, her coat glowing like burnished gold in the morning sunlight, she stood sniffing the aroma of frying bacon wafting on the breeze. Either that or she had come to warn me not to play with her little boy.

We crowded onto the side stoop. With enviable insouciance, graceful as a knock-kneed ballerina with pigeon toes, she glided down the driveway, across the lawn and around the corner. Graciously, the assembled family agreed that I must, indeed, have seen a moose.

"Some'un's puttin' out scraps. Smart t'ings dey is. Dey knows."

"Yis, I 'spects so. Yer're right dere, deys smart t'ings."

In one fell swoop, I had seen not only one, but two, moose and had contributed to the family folklore. Already I had heard them in the living room asking the newcomers, " 'Ear what 'appened t'Lara dis marnin'?"

Smiling smugly, I thought to myself, "Smart t'ings indeed! Never underestimate a moose, nor a mainlander."

Home Sweet Home

Escazú, Costa Rica, 1992

"Memsahib!"

"Señora!"

"Fraulein!"

"Madame!"

"Lady!"

" 'ey, Meesteh! Wan' change dollah?"

"I look car, yes?"

"Whud you wan'? Yes, yes, we 'ave. Sorry, is finish."

"Señora, this stamp is missing. Please, you stand in the long line over there. We are not giving this stamp today. Next week is Holy Week and many are away. You come back after."

"Good Morning. We have more passengers than seats on this flight; we can offer you..."

Stop!

In Canada, this would not happen. In Canada, this would be so simple to do. In Canada, no one will stare at me. In Canada, I could... I want to go home.

Home. Where is home? What is home anyway? Wherever it is, it's probably not Walton's Mountain, so why this overwhelming urge to go there?

More than a physical place, it is a place where you are protected from the stress of being faced with the unfamiliar or the threatening. It is a place where you know what is expected and what to expect, where one can bask in the comfort of a common culture—or sub-culture at least—and speak a familiar language. It is a place where you do not have to explain who you are, or what your job is, or where you are from. [Equally, it is a place where you can have no secrets, where you are known down to your last wart.]

The apron strings of the maternal hearth loosen with the approach of maturity and independence. They stretch apparently endlessly during the early flush of adulthood and grow loose during one's employment years. The onset of stiffening joints and shoulder twinges, however, seems to coincide with a re-tautening of the ties to the sights and sounds of youth. The apron strings start twitching again, hauling one in while the pursuit of what was, or what might have been, begins. A version of the homing instinct sets in.

A few people realize where they belong early in life and never leave home in the first place. Some venture away only to return when they settle down, start a family. Not so in the Foreign Service. For whatever reasons, this group of people succumbs to the lure of exotic places and a wandering life. Eventually though, even the most peripatetic succumb to the homing instinct and begin nesting, surrounding themselves with the objects, services and people which bring about the feelings of familiarity and belonging that create a home. Homing may lead to an actual return to birth roots, or to headquarters, or to a foreign home in countries that welcome retired diplomats with their pensions and access to foreign hard currency.

The Foreign Service is not the only wandering tribe of Canadians. Every consular officer has dealt with at least one member of the frustratingly eccentric Canadian expatriate community. In their search for home, these people fled the irritation of Canadian government regulation by investing in bureaucratically friendly Costa Rica, Ireland or Portugal; escaped the pressures of bilingualism by retiring to a condo in Puerto Rico [where they often live as Anglophones amid a Spanish speaking population]; or fled the discomfort of increased immigration by becoming an immigrant themselves. Embassy staff avoid looking too closely at this latter group lest they find themselves looking into a mirror. Homing to a third country is chancy at best and doomed to failure in the long run. When their health and wealth start to run out, most head back to Canada.

The energy required to adjust to constant change becomes harder to generate as one's age increases. Despite the acquisition of skills at cultural adaptation and language learning, the desire to live in a familiar milieu, to speak a familiar language, to be oneself, to have a shared and accepted history with one's community all coalesce into the decision to settle down at "home".

Whether it is age, marriage, money, divorce or retirement that initiates this homing instinct, the motivation is the same. Humans are social creatures with a fundamental need to belong to a group, to know their place in it, and to participate in the activities of that group. The group provides security. On a personal level, it is the security of familiar ways; on a larger scale, it provides security from outside threat—the threat that comes from not being understood. As with most ghetto professions, foreign service work like policing, priesting and politicking is never going to be understood by outsiders so we may as well ignore that as a motivation for going back to our roots.

Life in the Foreign Service brings a refinement in this dynamic that borders on the absurd. Once removed from the broader Canadian social context and shoved into a revolving-door system of home again - gone again, the group to which one belongs becomes very small. So small, in fact, it takes on aspects of a pre-industrial tribe in which adherence to artificial codes and mores becomes essential to survival and in which habit becomes law. This group, with its artificial homogeneity becomes, over the course of a thirty-five year career, the one in which Foreign Service people are most comfortable.

The prongs of homing are twofold. Firstly, although the Foreign Service community does offer the comfort of familiarity, it no longer provides protection from outside threat. As a respected segment of the public service, members of the Foreign Service used to be secure in their job prospects, could reasonably expect regular advancement and were able to retire on an adequate pension. This is no longer true. The group is divided, demoralized and at odds with itself, intent on individual survival and vulnerable to outside manipulation. Group members are not as mutually supporting as in years past. The number of career diplomats is decreasing as lateral entries, late entry and political entries increase. Nevertheless, any decision to leave the group is tantamount to another posting. And so, Ottawa, Kingston, Victoria, Vancouver and Montreal have become retirement enclaves for aging diplomats.

Secondly, a career of roaming the globe, peering through someone else's cultural glasses tends to warp one's eyesight and skew one's thinking. For better or worse is moot. You no longer think like people who stayed put. How many times did you have to bite your tongue on your last home leave? If you did not, how many times did you put your foot in your mouth? Diplomatic foot and mouth disease, going home can cause grievous bodily harm to the unwary. Granted, there are those who can spend half a lifetime abroad and then return home to Lower Shubenacadie, NS, without blinking an eye or feeling an intellectual pinch. For most of us, however, returning to the ancestral home in older age is risky business. We no longer belong.

Thus, when the homing instinct strikes, people of the Foreign Service find themselves hoist on their own petard. Seeking a life of change, that is what they have achieved. Unlike your goods in storage, although even there time is inexorable; everything we left behind went about changing, too. While our books acquired silverfish and our carpets grew mildew, relatives and friends moved away, the old neighbourhood expanded and the corner grocery closed.

Home. Where is home? Where do I feel at home? That is the question.

Great size does not protect Canada from the realities of global dynamics – migration, armed conflict, depleted resources, natural catastrophes, economic dependency — and modern information services make sure everyone shares the good news. Even the mind-numbing balm of CNN newscasts cannot prevent the spread of information. This is bad news for those who want to stop the world and get off. You cannot outrun change.

Neither can you avoid the consequences of being in the Foreign Service. Those who never leave home will always be wary of those who do. No one, except other colleagues or your Mother, wants to hear your stories. You can go home, but you cannot turn back time.

On the other hand, I have frequently been surprised at how very small the world has become.

Last week, we had a house guest from Canada, not an official one, just an ordinary woman, a teacher from Sackville, NB. It was the culmination of another apparently random series of events. First, the earthquake. Not the one that ripped apart the residence, the next one, the one that raised the east coast of Costa Rica by a meter and a half. Of the many people adversely affected were the students of a small school in which the computer room was destroyed. As it happened, these students were paired through electronic mail and the good graces of the Fundación Omar Dengi with a Canadian school. And where is this Canadian school? In the village where some of my family live. And who happens to be the Canadian teacher? A woman from New Delhi with whom we have acquaintances in common.

And then what happened? The myriad of previously invisible threads began to come together. The Canadian children raised money to help the Costa Rican students; the Canada Fund gave money to help the school; the Canadian teacher came to visit Costa Rica, and the Costa Rican teacher came to San José. Both of them stayed with us as house guests. When one afternoon we went downtown to explore the market area, I was struck by a sense of déja vu. I had done this very thing in every city I ever called home, whether in Ottawa or Nairobi or San José—take houseguests sightseeing. Three women from disparate countries, comfortable with each other, discussing education, childhood issues and their plans for expanding the computer connection between the students in Sackville with the students in Limón. In small ways we were doing what we could to break down barriers. I felt good, even if I was only a facilitator. For the moment, I felt comfortable, at home.

Yet, it was not my home, not where I belonged.

If I were at "home", that is if I were in Canada, what would be different? Would I know the streets any better? Could I speak to people any easier? Would more people know me? Would I fit in any better? Would "Me" be any different? Would going home now solve problems or merely replace old ones?

Recently I went home for a visit. Nothing was changed; yet all was changed. There was a strangeness to the familiarity. I looked as though I fit but my mind did not fit.

This question of home is complicated. Ultimately, I want to live where I feel that I belong.

It will take time, and I may come home a stranger, but put an October-blue sky over my head or a spring crocus under my window sill, and I know where I belong. Occasionally I want to be able to breathe the invigorating crisp northern air and say, "Ahh, this is a Canadian day."

Moving home will not solve problems nor bring an end to daily irritations, but I am very glad it is there waiting for me — not just yet, but someday. And if there is at least one grey-haired colleague to swap stories with, I will be content.

OTTAWA : 1992 – 2000

After returning to headquarters from Central America, we decided to remain in Ottawa as long as we could. As it transpired, that was for the rest of our foreign service life. My husband, in accepting a position in the Consular Affairs branch, ended up with the position of a lifetime. It was not considered a plum job, in fact, quite the opposite; however, it was a matter of turning lemons into lemon pie and enjoying the results which he did for the rest of his career.

Consular work, briefly, refers to the Canadian government's assistance to its citizens outside of the country who find themselves in a situation where they cannot help themselves, anything from lost passports, medical emergencies, death abroad, natural disasters, civil unrest, arrest, legal jeopardy to kidnapping. Diplomacy is government to government interaction usually leading to agreement on how to conduct relations between their countries on a broad front; consular is using these government to government channels to help individuals. It is the personal face of diplomacy. One that most Canadians so not know exists, let alone understand, until they are deep in trouble.

A grandfather visiting Africa strays from his tour group and is lost; consular people on the ground organize searches and inquiries until he is found or all options are exhausted. Three workers of a Canadian Company in South America are kidnapped for ransom; consular people work with local officials to determine where they are held and spearhead negotiations for their successful release. A mother's son hasn't been heard from in two weeks; consular people contact local police, hospitals, contacts and find him in a hostel hundreds of kilometres from where is supposed to be and restore him to his family's bosom. And then there are the larger issues of illegal rendition, international child kidnapping, Canadians in foreign jails, natural disasters, plane crashes and civil unrest involving Canadians abroad. These crises all land on the desks of consular officials and depend on the cooperation of foreign governments for satisfactory resolution.

Successful consular works also depends on the will of the home government to support its citizens abroad and, for this period at least, the Canadian government supported the efforts of its consular people at home and overseas.

Coming Dear

Over the years I have held more than a few offices. Two of them were that of secretary and, later, president of the Foreign Service Community Association. The FSCA has been in existence since 1983. It is open to anyone interested in the rotational foreign service life and offers a range of services to make that life easier. Most families and many singles are members. It also consults and advises the department on issues that involve family members of rotational personnel at headquarters and overseas. Occasionally I was asked to make a speech. The following is a version of one such effort delivered fifteen years ago. Perhaps such speeches and articles have assisted to improve the conditions of service for people in the Canadian Foreign Service.

At the time this speech was made, I was employed outside of Foreign Affairs and ready to have a life of my own rather than continue as a tagalong spouse to my husband's career, so, at the end of my term as President, I resigned and have had little to do with foreign service life since.

Ottawa, October, 1994

October was Women's History Month. One of the events arranged by External Affairs and International Trade Canada (EAITC) was a panel discussion entitled "The Evolving Role and Contribution of Women". The topic begs the question, "Has the role of women in the department evolved?" Evolution implies the arrival of a more advanced state. The role has changed but the evolution, or the revolution if you will, continues. The definitive state has yet to be reached.

Personal experience, especially emotion-charged experience, colours any analysis of that experience. Ripping heart and hearth away from home and plunging into the minefield of a foreign culture is an emotion-charged experience and, therefore, every assessment of the positive and negative aspects of the changing role of women in the foreign service will bear this personal stamp. In this case, it reflects not only my experience but my mood of the moment. Also, my role has been as a family member and occasional contract worker, not as a permanent employee.

The women of External Affairs and International Trade Canada (EAITC) comprise a diverse group of people, each with their own perspective on their role and status. The only commonalities for the group are rotationality and femaleness. Otherwise they may be employee or dependent, married or single, English or French, Canadian or foreign-born, officer or support staff, with children or without, young or mature, home-maker or career person.

As Canadian women explored the advantages and disadvantages of the Women's Movement, they brought pressure to bear on the government, their employers and their lovers to respond to their right to equality with men, equal opportunity for employment, equal pay for equal work and equal freedom to choose their path in life. EAITC, as an employer and quasi-paterfamilias, is a cumbersome antiquated bureaucracy, struggling reluctantly to adapt to a changing world. It has, albeit somewhat reluctantly, accepted its responsibility towards rotational families and carried out this responsibility in light of what it felt was good for them. In the early days, the department decided what was good for the families and did it, now it agrees that change is needed and slowly moves in that direction. It is learning to listen and is becoming more responsive.

Probably the largest subgroup of women affected by employment in the foreign service are those who accompany rotational employees to post as dependent spouses, the ones that used to be referred to as "wives". Another speaker will address the issues that arise from being a woman employee within the Department. Twenty-five years ago, the majority of women in the foreign service were there as wives, therefore, any spousal issue was interpreted as a "wives" issue and treated as a tempest in a teapot, that is to say, with less than due diligence. That this is no longer true does not mean there are fewer wives. It does mean that the group is more heterogeneous and the issues have changed to reflect that diversity. Women's issues have become family issues, spousal issues that include women and men as accompanying spouses, child-rearing issues, female employee issues, family issues acknowledging nuclear families and single parent families, foreign born spouses, same-sex spouses, commuter families, single employee issues and so on. The definition of family has broadened and diversified and so have the departmental responses begun to adapt to the new reality.

Once Upon a Time

Let's look at where we were. The role of the traditional wife revolved around homemaking, child rearing, community volunteer work, home hospitality and the nurture of family relations. This role changed very little for most wives when they were posted abroad. It did, and still does, take considerable creativity to solve everyday childcare and home management problems in a foreign culture. The specifics change from country to country, but the role does not change and, in fact, remains much the same as it was at home.

For women married to officers there was the additional role of representational hospitality, both giving and receiving, which at the senior levels was quite onerous: social gatherings, good works, expatriate out-reach, TLC for distressed Canadians, Commonwealth associations, diplomatic ladies' clubs and representational lunches and dinners to give and attend. It was assumed that the wives would accept this representational role; not only accept it, but embrace it, expand it and glory in it, carrying out with style and grace (and for free) a major public relations campaign on behalf of the Canadian government. In fact, until the early 70's, there was a line or two on every officer's evaluation form that asked for an assessment of the wife's ability in this regard.

Along the way from then to now, this representational role has fallen into limbo, if not disrepute. It used to be that if one did it well, it was recognized by the community, and the respect it gathered was almost enough to make it worthwhile. It took a lot of respect and silent congratulations to compensate for the inroads it made into one's privacy, family life and individual freedom. Gradually, it became obvious that fulfilling one's representational duties was irrelevant to the department, to the advancement of the employee's career or to a woman's status in her group. In keeping with societal changes, departmental wives turned to success in the workforce to gain both self-respect and the respect of other women. Not to say it was not done, it just slipped into something one did, not something one gloried in. And the use of local restaurants increased dramatically, as did the use of the business lunch instead of the full five course diplomatic dinner.

Women need the respect of other women, too, and being able to host a formal dinner with its seating plans and hand written menus no longer cuts it. Also, in Canadian society, respect can no longer be earned through vicarious enjoyment of the status of one's husband. I'm talking respect here, not sycophancy. Women want to earn their own right to respect and privilege. Unfortunately, foreign service wives find that their freedom of choice still runs smack up against the confines of a rotational service, just as it always has. It sticks right in our faces such questions as, "How much am I willing to sacrifice for my own career?", "Can we afford to buy a house if I stop working to accompany my spouse overseas?", "Which is more important to me, my marriage or my career?"

Respect at this point in time appears to be tied firmly to paid work outside the home. The right and wrong of this situation is another issue that is evolving, rapidly, I hope. Choice is the goal; the freedom to choose is what is important. We should be so lucky as to have a life that offers us the opportunity to choose and then have the societal freedom to choose what we will regardless of gender.

Win, Lose or Draw

On a personal level, after twenty-five years as a foreign service spouse, the question for me now is, "Where did I start and where am I now in relation to where I expected to be?" In other words, "Have I lost or gained by life in the foreign service?" Have I reached any conclusions after twenty-five years in the foreign service? Would I rather have done something else?

Two things are key to determining positive or negative outcomes: goals and choices. I suspect that most of us who married young or right out of university did not really have firm goals for our lives. Our goals evolved as we matured, saw more of life and its options, gained in experience and became aware of our own strengths and weaknesses. For many of us, our goals and interests may not have become apparent until we had our first or even second posting overseas. Thanks to the feminist movement, this is a time when most women are questioning their life paths so it is not surprising that foreign service women are doing the same.

A foreign service wife has certain choices already made for her; her life is going to include repeated postings, and she will have very little control over where and when they will be or what they will entail. So any choice automatically includes an element of change that makes long term planning tentative. In pre-posting briefings, I tell participants quite frankly that if they cannot cope with the demands of repeated overseas assignments, they and their family should do some serious thinking about their choice of employment.

No life offers any guarantees, so I feel that to blame the foreign service for unfulfilled expectations or unattained goals is to refuse to take responsibility for oneself. I had not realized this fully until recently. Consequently, my only regret is that I failed to identify some situations as opportunities, choosing to consider them obstacles instead. The loss is mine and I regret them.

After years of associating primarily with foreign service people from our own country and from others, I now spend my time with people, many of them retired, who have spent most of their adult lives in the same place, the same place being in and around Ottawa or the Ottawa Valley. Their foreign experience consists mainly of visits to ethnic restaurants and a little touring. Their lives have contained as many disappointments as mine and they never left home. I am not a Board of Education Trustee, nor a Supervisor of Schools, nor even a high school principal which is what I set out to be. Would I have been had I remained in Canada? I'll never know and I don't care. I have climbed a cliff in the Khyber Pass and breathed the dust of a camel caravan with the shade of Alexander the Great. I have watched a hundred elephants silently pass my tent through the fog of a Kenyan dawn. I have spent Christmas on a beach and New Year's on a mountain top. I have shaken hands with Presidents and street sellers and felt sweat on the hands of both. I have received an education not available to most people and shared the learning with my family; I have built a storehouse of memories to entertain my old age.

I would not have had it any other way.

Fifty Years and Counting

Ottawa, April 1, 1999

In commemoration of the union of Canada with Newfoundland and Labrador, we invited friends to a Screech-In and general good Newfie Time. There were no seal flippers, turrs or stuffed squid; however, there was fish and salt beef, pease pudding and spotted Dick washed down with tots of rum and strong tea. What with all the toasting and general hilarity, the rollicking went on until the next day.

The Siren Sea

The sea lore called them…
And the sea lord claimed them.
Yet still they came.
St. Brendan the Navigator,
The sons of Oden and Thor,
The children of Gaul.
They found no gold nor passage,
But in the deep Atlantic rage,
They found the Fish.
The Fish, with barbeled chin
And slimy mottled skin.
A million million tons they took.
Salt-bound for Spain,
Barbados, out and home again.
The Fish made some men rich.
Others paid the price
To the Rock, the sea and the ice.
They endured for the fish.
And when they'd won,
The ocean mine was done,
The final harvest run.
The sea oil calls them…
And the sea lord claims them,
Yet still they come.